The Inspiring Story of Will Shakespeare's Life

Befriend *the* Bard!

PAMELA HOWARTH

authorHOUSE

AuthorHouse™ UK
1663 Liberty Drive
Bloomington, IN 47403 USA
www.authorhouse.co.uk
Phone: 0800.197.4150

Published by AuthorHouse 10/14/2016

ISBN: 978-1-5246-3755-2 (sc)
ISBN: 978-1-5246-3756-9 (hc)
ISBN: 978-1-5246-3754-5 (e)

Illustrations by Richard Buxton
www.richardbuxtonart.com

Print information available on the last page.

In memory of my mother

who read and enjoyed this book in its early stages.

Peggy Blunson 1922-2015

Contents

Mr. WILLIAM

SHAKESPEARES

COMEDIES,
HISTORIES, &
TRAGEDIES.

Published according to the True Originall Copies.

LONDON
Printed by Isaac Iaggard, and Ed. Blount. 1623

Title page of the First Folio edition of Shakespeare's plays, 1623.

30 SECOND BIOGRAPHY

Will Shakespeare left his home, wife and children, sometime between the years 1585 and 1592, to seek his fortune in London. He became an actor, playwright and theatre-manager at just the right time, when drama as an art form was really taking off. As a member of a highly successful company of players, he regularly entertained royalty at court, as well as the public in the newly built theatres. He quickly became established as their in-house writer, and completed thirty-seven plays (plus a few collaborations), comprising a mix of comedies, tragedies and histories. He also wrote five long poems and 154 sonnets. He eventually returned to his family in Stratford, where he died in 1616.

Much of his life is still a mystery today and likely to remain so.

Mystery Man

Will's exact date of birth isn't known, but it's not the only mystery about him...

In no particular order, I've jotted down 20 questions which have puzzled me about Will Shakespeare. There are many more:

1. What did he look like?
2. How did he pronounce his name?
3. Was he a secret Catholic?
4. What was his relationship with his wife, Anne?
5. Was he intending to marry another woman?
6. Was he faithful to his wife?
7. Was he bisexual?
8. What happened to him in the *lost years?*
9. Did he go to Lancashire as a tutor?
10. Why and when did he go to London?
11. Did his family ever visit him in London or see one of his plays?
12. Did he ever go to Italy or travel *anywhere* abroad?
13. Did he have some kind of mid-life crisis or nervous breakdown?
14. Did he ever intend his sonnets to be published?
15. Who was the *fair youth, Mr W.H.?*
16. Who was *the dark lady?*
17. Why did he buy the Blackfriars house in London?
18. Did he have an illegitimate son?
19. Did he write the curse on his grave and has anyone ever defied it and moved his bones?
20. In his will, why does he itemize the *second-best bed?*

PROLOGUE: Who was Will?

This isn't an easy question to answer, partly due to lack of hard evidence, partly due to time, and partly, I believe, due to the essential nature of the man called William Shakespeare. I have a feeling that even to his contemporaries – friends, family, lovers, theatre people, wealthy patrons and all the others he met – he was a bit of an enigma, a dark horse, a mystery man with many faces. He played lots of different parts in his life – as we all do – but, being a professional actor, he was probably extremely good at it and could assume different roles *at will*. (Pun intended – the Elizabethans loved puns and wordplay.)

He could also hide behind his writing. As a professional dramatist, Will wrote to entertain audiences, telling stories that would be enacted on a stage, *but never speaking directly in his own voice.* Today most people know more about the plots of well-known plays, like *Romeo and Juliet*, than they do about Will's own fascinating life or the kind of person he was.

Will, the man, stands in the shadows, off-stage, as it were, behind his plays, the dauntingly huge body of writing we know as *The Complete Works of Shakespeare,* now so famous that they are going viral, as we speak. It's a bit of a miracle that we have them at all, but more about that in due course…

If more of The Immortal Bard's personal writing had survived – if, for example, there were some letters, diary entries, ideas scribbled on a bar bill even – then we'd have more insight into his private life, thoughts and feelings, so that cracking the *Who-was-Will* conundrum would be easier. But not a jot remains – *there's the rub* – except for the cryptic and much more personal sonnets which will keep readers guessing until the end of time.

In Will's day, only the lives of royalty and aristocrats were recorded for posterity: Will didn't belong to either group, though he certainly got to *mix* with courtiers, nobles and two monarchs during his career. Of course, no one could look into the seeds of time and see that his fame would last for centuries or that scholars would devote years of research to finding out more about him! He may have only been alive for 52 years, but his work lives on and on.

Most of the evidence supporting Will's life consists of public records like church and court documents, title deeds and tax returns: the Elizabethans were good at keeping meticulous records and an amazing number have survived. There are also some helpful comments from contemporaries, but the first biography wasn't written till years after Will's death, by which time no one was left who knew him, so some of the information was bound to be inaccurate, based on gossip and hearsay.

It's also sad for us, in the age of instant photography, that we have no idea what Will looked like for much of his life and that few authenticated likenesses remain, mainly ones made in later life. Everyone has a mental picture of an old-ish, balding dude with a pointy beard and a fancy Elizabethan collar, but what did he look like as a boy, or on his wedding day or as a young, successful actor-writer, his star rising in the theatre firmament?

No original drafts of the plays have survived, either, except possibly one, a few scenes from a play about Sir Thomas More, which current scholarship believes that Will wrote in collaboration with others, and which is thought to be in his handwriting. Apart from this, there are a few original signatures – and that is all.

Treasure-hunting for anything related to our Will has been going on for ages, with some success, but nothing yet that definitely answers the big questions or fills the yawning gaps. People have even dug up the graves of those who knew him, in the hope of finding bundles of letters or missing plays, though they've probably not dared to touch Will's grave, for reasons I'll come to. It's unlikely now that much more evidence will ever be found, but you never know: next time you're in an antique shop, or at a country house sale, you might discover some papers mouldering away in an old chest, long-forgotten documents and manuscripts, that could be worth a fortune and change the course of Shakespearean scholarship.

What's all the fuss about?

So, one of the many paradoxes about Will is that he is a national icon, the genius everyone knows, but the *man* no-one knows. His awesome reputation has grown throughout the centuries but as a person he's vague and insubstantial. It's only natural to wonder why the works of his pen are treated like Holy Writ, while the human being behind them seems to get lost in the religious worship, the apotheosis of *William Shakespeare*.

Who's all the fuss about?

What I'm trying to do in the pages of this book is to re-humanize him, which I hope will help those who are just discovering him to approach more confidently and *befriend* the Bard. As the actor, Al Pacino, has said: *What's this thing that gets between us and Shakespeare?* Probably the fear that his writing is too difficult, that we're not going to understand it. The intention of this book is to get past the works to the person who wrote them.

To help you make a start and get over the mental block, I want to bring Will, the man, into focus, to give you a feel for his life and times, and to put his plays into context, so that you can begin to understand, literally, where this mega-talented human being is coming from...

Birth

ACT ONE:

Childhood and Adolescence: 1564-1582

1. First the Infant, Mewling and Puking in His Mother's Arms

Will lived in an age which feels like the dim and distant past to us today, though we're very familiar with many of its images from books, film and TV. He came into this world in the middle of the 16th century, in the middle of England, in the middle of one of the most famous and turbulent periods of English history. He lived in eventful times between two incredible upheavals which affected everyone in society – the English Reformation and the English Civil War. In the first, the Roman Catholic religion was thrown out; in the second, the king was thrown out; revolution led to Charles I's execution and Britain became a commonwealth for a period of eleven years before the monarchy was restored under Charles II. You'll find these events in the history books, usually in a chapter headed *Tudors and Stuarts*.

Will was born in a town called Stratford-upon-Avon in Warwickshire, the post-code for Henley Street, where he lived, being CV37 6QW. You can visit it via Google Earth or travel there in reality, but I'll help you to visualise it as it was when Will was born, 450 years ago. Not, of course, that our playwright would have known anything about post codes, GPS signals, the Internet, or indeed, planes, cars and trains. Electricity hadn't been discovered, never mind about electronics: *candle-power* and *horsepower* meant just what they said. A *tablet* for an Elizabethan would have been a little scrunched together pile of folded paper.

Lots of things were pretty vague – measurements, spelling rules, the calendar... The map of the world was incomplete and often wrong; the planetary system was little understood, all mixed up with astrological tables and superstitious beliefs. Having said this, the theory of the earth being the centre of the universe was about to be discredited, and new studies recognised that our planet in fact orbited the sun. The earth, itself, was being explored at a vast rate of knots – literally – as huge sailing ships went on voyages of exploration to chart the waters and find new lands, like

America. Terrestrial globes were being crafted for the first time and must have been as wonderful in their time as the telephone has been for us. Great changes were afoot and new discoveries were being made by brilliant men: it's always tempting to think of people from history as being less intelligent than we are, but the more you discover about the Elizabethans, the more you realise that this was far from true. They probably felt they were living in a *brave new world*, (one of Will's multitude of new-minted phrases still in use today), much as we do now, with the rapid pace of technology affecting our lives at every turn.

Apart from the lack of technology that we take for granted, people in the 16th century weren't so different: they probably felt pretty much as we do about the bedrock essentials of the human condition, running the same gamut of emotions, and being motivated by the same driving forces that make us what we are today. They needed to love and be loved, they valued family and friends, they, no doubt, had goals and aspirations; they battled with the problems of life, just as we do, only probably more desperately, because life was very tough for most of them.

Even though the country under Elizabeth I was called *Merry England* by historians, it wasn't very merry at all for the majority of the population. Some people were extremely clever and learned, while many were totally uneducated and couldn't even write their names, including, it is thought, Will's parents. There was a huge gulf between the haves and have-nots, the nobles or upper classes and all the rest. The former were often extremely rich, while most of the latter were very poor, struggling to feed themselves, though a new middle class of merchants and prosperous tradesmen was beginning to emerge. Many, both rich *and* poor, died young; without modern medicines, one in ten survived to be forty, and only a few made old bones. The majority of people were deeply religious, holding strong Christian beliefs about life after death, believing in hell (along with witches, demons and fairies) and hoping that they would go to heaven; for many this represented the promise of a much better world than the one they lived in on earth. As you will discover, religious doctrine and practices were a key part of life – religion rules, ok – though they were far from fixed or settled, along with so many other things.

But to go back to the town of William Shakespeare's birth, Stratford-on-Avon, in the heart of England... If you happen to visit, you'll be directed by brown heritage signs to the Birthplace Museum. You'll cross the river by Clopton Bridge with its views towards the Royal Shakespeare Theatre, and walk into town, past timber-framed buildings, including, nowadays, High Street chains, numerous gift shops selling souvenirs and the ubiquitous cafes, restaurants and pubs. In Henley Street, you'll find a house, prettied up with well-tended gardens, where Will was, *almost certainly,* born and in which, it's known that he grew up.

Not much is *completely certain* about the life of Will Shakespeare. You can get the dry facts from a website but, given the lack of evidence already mentioned, these only offer sketchy information without much narrative or context; I hope I can paint in some of the hinterland to Will's life-story to give you a bigger and more colourful picture. But at times you'll have to make up your own mind about what actually happened from several versions, often conflicting ones, rather like a multiple choice questionnaire, with no right answers. *On the one hand...on the other hand* sentences will be common. I'll help you separate fact from fiction but you'll require a bit of imagination, too, just as the *first* audiences did when they watched Will's plays in the *first* London theatres all those years ago.

If you climb the stairs up to the main bedchamber in the Shakespeare family home, now the Birthplace Museum, you'll find the room furnished much as it would have been in the spring of 1564 when Mary Shakespeare was anxiously awaiting the birth of her third child, after two previous children, both girls, had died as babies. With a bit of imagination, you can invent a few details. Perhaps it's night time, perhaps the street is silent, or perhaps a light April shower beats against the casement window. Perhaps the moon and stars are unusually bright, the planets aligned significantly, portending the birth of a rare soul.

Mary may be murmuring prayers – whether Roman Catholic or Protestant prayers, we don't know – she may not know either because the country has gone through such religious turmoil. It doesn't matter when you're desperate.

Please God, let the child live. Please God, a strong, healthy child this time...

The crib is ready once again and the strips of fabric to swaddle the new-born are washed and laid out in hope of a living baby. Dawn comes up over the horizon, creeping through the Forest of Arden, bathing the river in surreal light and waking the townsfolk. They haven't got clocks in their houses but it doesn't really matter. Having no electricity means they have to work from dawn to dusk, when there is light.

Please, let the child thrive this time. Please God, a healthy child for us...

Imagine her friend, Judith, busying herself below in the kitchen, making a cordial, a herbal brew, said to ease the pain of labour. With Mary in her hour of need, there are unlikely to be any men – just female relatives or friends, though her husband, John, probably waits anxiously downstairs as the labour progresses Childbirth is women's business and a risky one too, with high maternal and infant mortality rates. The local midwife may have been called – a woman who knows some tricks to ease the baby's passage into the world, but is powerless to do much if it gets stuck or if the mother haemorrhages.

Holy Mary, be with me in my travail! By all the saints, don't let this child die a-borning!

All Mary's prayers are answered. Seven years after her marriage, the expected baby, her first son, enters the world, destined to live.

Shakespeare's birth place, Henley Street, Stratford-upon-Avon. Now the Birthplace Museum.

Gulielmus, filius Johannes Shakespeare

We know that very soon after his birth, the baby was christened *William* and recorded as the *son of John Shakespeare* in the parish register, kept by law, in the church of Holy Trinity, which you can still see today if you visit Stratford. The entry is in Latin, because that was the language of the church, the law and most official documents. The date is the 26th April, 1664. Most babies were baptised very soon after birth because so many died in the first days, weeks and months of life. The strong religious belief from the old Catholic religion was that the soul of a child, if it died, would then go to heaven, whereas, unbaptized, it would wander in Purgatory eternally. A kind of insurance policy, then, and some sort of solace for the bereaved parents.

From this parish record, researchers and historians have guessed that William's birth was probably a few days or so before, placing it on or around the 23rd April, *but we don't know for sure.* As the 23rd is St George's Day, England's patron saint's day, it feels appropriate somehow to call this Will's birthday; it has been kept ever since and each anniversary is celebrated to this day in the streets of Stratford with performances and processions.

Not only did the new baby, Will, thrive in that spring of 1564, but he also survived an outbreak of plague in Stratford. Just after the record of Will's baptism, on the same page, is a grim statement, *Hic Incipit pestis,* or *Here beginneth plague.* There follows a long, sad list of all the townsfolk from Stratford, over 200 of them, men, women and children, who perished in the epidemic of this horrific disease. Will and his parents were lucky and stayed healthy, though they were no doubt very fearful, especially as they had already lost two children.

If you survived childhood, you were lucky; so many youngsters never made it to adulthood and medicine was very primitive. It relied mainly on herbal remedies, which could sometimes be effective, and a practice called bleeding, which wasn't. Blood was taken from the patient in the belief that the illness was being let out of the body, which usually only succeeded in weakening the sufferer even more. Sorcery and spells, together with prayers, were the only other options. However, more accurate knowledge was being learnt about human biology and Harvey's discovery of the circulation of the blood by the heart was only a few years in the future.

The comparatively simple old world was turning and the newly-born Will was going to have to face very different challenges from any his parents could have imagined.

2. Will's family

As the firstborn child to survive, and the oldest son, Will was probably very special to his parents, John and Mary Shakespeare, who were comparatively prosperous tradespeople, part of the new rising middle class in England at the time. They were most likely illiterate, as already mentioned, which seems incredible for the parents of a writer who was to become world-famous. Their business was the making and selling of gloves-- not only practical, but also highly fashionable items of clothing-- and other leather goods. There are also references to John's dealing in corn and wool, and to the fact that he might have also been a butcher.

Stratford in those days numbered about 2000 inhabitants and was an important market town. Not many years later, the newly built theatres in London, where Will's plays were acted, would accommodate *at least that number in the audience at one performance,* but his parents weren't to know this. They were only grateful that, much to everyone's relief, the baby had come through the ordeal of birth, as had his mother, who went on to have five more children, Will's brothers and sisters. One little girl, Anne, died when she was eight. The others survived to become adults though most of them were to die very young by today's standards. The only other girl, the child who lived the longest, Joan, was named for one of the first dead babies, as was often customary in families. All the rest were boys: Gilbert, Richard and finally Edmund, born when Will was sixteen. The cradle was in constant use and the house on Henley Street soon filled up with children and their noise.

You'll have to imagine the young toddler, Will, learning to talk, prattling away with ease, loving the sounds of the words, repeating them over and over as children do. Like many kids, he probably invented words of his own, a private language, but for Will the ability to make up new words, diverting himself with non-standard vocabulary, never left him, but fed into everything he wrote, to the enrichment of the English language. It is said that he added over 1500 new words (neologisms) to English, including compound words and familiar words given a make-over as different parts of speech. Many have survived to this day, along with phrases which have become so familiar that we don't think twice about them.

I thought I'd use one of them, **in my mind's eye**, for the purely imaginative sections of Will's story. Another familiar phrase originally coined by Will, **in a nutshell**, could be useful when I want to write brief notes on key, need-to-know topics. If I want to pause the story for a moment to give my take on something, I could say **methinks**, the Elizabethan way of saying simply *I think*...

So – *methinks* – Will must have enjoyed the old rhymes that adults have always recited for the young down the centuries, savouring the rhythms and the rhyming words, as children do. In an age with no way of recording music, he'd listen to the lyrics and tunes of the old songs sung by his mother or those around him, and he'd develop his love of music from hearing the *catches, glees* and ballads which were performed at most convivial occasions when a good sing-song was enjoyed by all, usually along with wine or beer. He'd be fascinated, as children are, by stories told by those around him, in a world heavily dependent on oral and aural tradition, because most people didn't know how to read or write the stories down. He probably remembered everything he heard, mopping it up like a sponge. *Methinks* he'd pick up all the gossip coming in through the door of the shop with the customers and was, no doubt, the sort of child who often embarrassed the adults with his forwardness and sharp ear for things he wasn't supposed to hear, let alone repeat. All children go through a very imaginative phase so I think it's safe to say that Will had a wonderful inner life and fantasy world he could live in when he chose. Again, the difference was that it never left him in maturity, but could be drawn on again and again in his writing.

Did John and Mary realise that they had an exceptional child? Well, probably, yes. Most parents have a pretty good instinct about these things, though Will's parents wouldn't see his particular talents as those of genius, in the way that, say, a child prodigy like Mozart could be recognised two centuries later. Will's particular gifts had yet to mature. John and Mary undoubtedly realised that young Will had a fertile imagination, often called *fancy* then, but so had most children, hadn't they? It's likely that they soon knew their son to be a quick learner who would benefit from an education. Even in the midst of their busy hardworking lives, with mouths to feed, did they look at the young Will, their firstborn, and wonder? *Perchance to dream* of a great future for him?

In most ways Will's family was no different outwardly from others in Stratford, though probably more comfortable than many. At a time when nearly everyone had a large family because of a lack of any reliable contraception, most homes were crowded: it's difficult for us to imagine now the almost total lack of privacy which was part of existence, especially in a house which was also a business and shop. Personal space, as we know it today, was a luxury way in the future: the kind of *private time/ down-time/me-time* – whatever you want to call it – was only for the very rich or those with small families. Most people led pretty hum-drum lives where there was little peace and quiet, and day to day living, consisted of hard, relentless work, leisure being a rare pleasure. Children would make their own entertainment and invent games, just as they always have. There wouldn't be many toys or books – certainly no books for children – and most unlettered families, like Will's, would probably only own a prayer book and a Bible.

At the time of Will's birth, his dad, John, was doing very nicely, thank you. He'd been born to a tenant farming family in a village and married Mary Arden, the daughter of the farm owners, so a good match there, then. Mary was also linked – distantly – to the aristocratic family which gave its name to the local expanse of woodland, the Forest of Arden, so possibly her parents were none too pleased about their daughter's marrying beneath her socially. On the other hand, John Shakespeare was showing every sign of becoming a self-made man: not content with working the land, he had moved into Stratford and set up as a glove seller and manufacturer. It may sound a rather cushy number but it had involved a long apprenticeship of several years, as learning most skilled crafts and trades did: he would have been known as a *whittawer,* a glove-maker who could make the most expensive white kid gloves as part of his craft.

Running his own business meant doing everything from buying the animal hides, sometimes slaughtering the animals himself, to preparing the skins and then cutting and sewing them into gloves. Making hides supple enough for sewing involved the intensive labour of soaking them in all sorts of noxious substances including urine – and sometimes dog-poo. Not a pleasant and fragrant way to earn a living! The workshop, stores and shop were almost certainly part of the family home, so Will would have grown up in this rather smelly environment.

Having said that, with an almost total lack of sewage and drainage systems, most Elizabethans were used to much more smelly conditions than we are today, especially in the towns. At best they had a basic outside hole-in-the-ground toilet, or privy, and at worst human waste was often emptied onto a stinking muck-hill in the street. From legal documents we know that John Shakespeare was at one time fined for having one outside his house! It's incredible how we can know trivial details like this centuries later but still have no idea what England's greatest playwright did for many key years of his life! The reason lies in the detailed documentation kept in Elizabethan England – of court cases from petty offences to major crimes, as well as records of births, marriages and deaths. It's pure chance what survives and what doesn't, but it's mainly from this kind of paper-trail that experts have assiduously pieced together the known facts of Will's life.

So, stench and all, Will probably knew his father's trade inside out, and, as the eldest son, was no doubt expected to help with some of the work or to go on errands, collecting hides from local farmers or delivering gloves to customers. It's likely, too, that he started to acquire a feel for the financial side of things and to develop the shrewd business sense that would be an asset to him in later life. Methinks Will was a chip off the old block in money matters and probably in aspects of his personality, too; John must have been a confident, aspirational man, with a strong sense of self-belief, to have moved up the social scale as he did, and his son, Will, seems to have inherited these qualities.

Town and Country

Stratford people must have been proud of their town, especially its buildings like the Guildhall, the church and the grand bridge over the river. Like many similar towns, it was run by a corporation which had considerable powers of authority, though ultimately it was controlled by the Queen and her appointed ministers who issued orders which had to be obeyed. A democracy it was not: the Queen was an absolute ruler. She regularly sent officers across the country, a network of spies, to check up on the town councils to make sure everyone was doing her bidding. It was a world of social-policing, as we would call it now, where neighbours were encouraged to snitch on each other, reporting misdeeds to the authorities. You were reasonably safe so long as you stayed on the right side of the law and the Queen but, step over the line, and there was a harsh system of punishment in place.

In a Nutshell: Crime and Punishment

For crimes such as theft, poaching, adultery, blasphemy and non-attendance at church you could be fined and made to do public penance, but many punishments involved more brutal retribution like being whipped, put in the stocks or having parts of your anatomy cut off, like hands or ears. In Elizabethan England, you could be hanged for stealing something very small in value. Strict laws attached to vagrancy, too: no-one could travel to another town without a licence and beggars were literally whipped out of town if they didn't belong there. If they returned again they were branded and, the third time they were hanged.

There was one set of laws for the poor, another for the rich, who were usually only tried on more serious charges like murder, sedition, treason, inciting rebellion and so on. Punishment was again brutal, the worst kind of death sentence being hanging, drawing and quartering. Trials were often very unfair with the onus being on prosecution, not defence: if this wasn't bad enough, various gruesome methods of torture, like the rack, *the collar* and *the iron maiden*, were employed which could make anyone confess to anything, even if they were completely innocent

The Town Council

Will's father was for many years a model citizen. His business was prospering and he was soon able to buy property and land, a sure sign of success. He also wanted to play a part in the town's civic affairs and had by 1561 become a member of the corporation, as an alderman, then the Chamberlain (Treasurer) then, finally, High Bailiff – like our Mayor, though with more power. These were responsible positions, showing a strong sense of duty, as well as ability and leadership qualities. John Shakespeare must have been numerate and he'd probably learned to read in some degree, too, or he'd never have coped with all the work required for the town council. In the year of Will's birth, 1664, he was the official who authorised, possibly against his conscience, the obligatory smashing of the stained glass in the Guildhall at Stratford, one of the outward, visible signs of the Catholic religion which the state had rejected under Elizabeth.

At the height of his civic success, he decided to apply for a *grant of arms,* which would mean that he was entitled to have a family crest that could be handed down to his descendants. He must have been proud of his family – there were stories of ancestors who'd fought for king and country – and he probably felt that through his own efforts he'd made a substantial contribution to his town *and* to his family status, therefore deserving the title of *gentleman.* Upward mobility is not a new phenomenon – just a new name for the age-old desire to climb the social ladder, often through financial success. Unfortunately, nothing came of the application, though later, when Will became a successful playwright, it was a different story...

I can imagine Will and his brothers and sisters being proud of their dad – watching him go to town meetings, seeing him walk in processions, dressed in his robes. Some of his prestige must have attached to them, too, perhaps small privileges and acknowledgements in the town. *This is John Shakespeare's son*, someone might say, introducing Will, making him feel important and respected. Later, in London, Will was to see the glory of status on a much grander scale: indeed, it became one of the key themes in his plays. He was fascinated by human ambition and the roller-coaster ride of those who seek power, often losing it again through their own fault. But in Stratford, the microcosm of the state, he first watched his father's efforts to become *somebody* and knew, all too well, the brittle uncertainty of staying at the top once you'd arrived. The *bubble reputation* could so easily burst.

As he grew older and more independent, young Will would no doubt explore the fields and woods which surrounded the town. It was gentle, rolling countryside, still largely unspoilt today: no dramatic mountains or moors, the wild landscape of some parts of Britain. Roaming with friends or on his own, it was here that Will would have absorbed all the knowledge of nature around him which would later feed into his writing: he would learn the names of birds, trees and flowers, including, of course, their local dialect names. He was especially fond of wild flowers, as there are many descriptions of them his plays, for example Puck's speech, in *A Midsummer Night's Dream,* beginning:

I know a bank where the wild thyme blows, Where oxlips and the nodding violet grows…

If this speech sounds like a line from a perfect pastoral poem, there are many others in Will's plays describing *adverse* weather, storms and bitter cold, as Will painted the play's scenery in words for the audience to imagine.

England was a rural country, much of its land being given over to sheep-farming for wool and meat – but this occupation was far from being a bucolic idyll, more of a hand-to-mouth existence. Growing up, Will would no doubt have been sensitive to Nature and the beauty of the changing seasons, but he must also have been aware of the way the weather dominated the lives of those around him, literally making the difference between life and death. A poor harvest meant starvation for those who were dependent on the land, which was nearly everybody, the poorest, as usual, being the worst hit. Even today, in spite of advanced technology, we are vulnerable to extremes of climate, over which we have little control, and it is still usually the poorest who suffer most.

Will was to set many of his plays in far-away countries or imaginary states, but whether it's Italy or Illyria, Greece or Cyprus, most of the references to nature, farming and the landscape come from much closer to home, his innate knowledge of Warwickshire, acquired during his boyhood. One of the great mysteries of his life is whether he ever travelled abroad, whether he ever saw Venice or Rome or Verona, or whether he just read about them and used his fertile imagination.

Will probably spoke with a local accent, too, and I expect he was teased about his rustic origins when he got to London. He was probably all too aware that he was from a lower social class than the elite group of writers who dominated the scene when he first arrived. The story of Will Shakespeare was not exactly a rags to riches one, though, when he left for London, his family were far less prosperous than they had been, but the oft-told tale of the country boy who goes to the big city to pursue a dream and to make something of himself.

But I'm getting ahead of my story.

3. *In my mind's eye:* The School Run 1575

Young Will is making his way to school on a cold winter's morning after a breakfast of bread and weak ale. (Water wasn't safe to drink and there was no tea, coffee or juice.) He has some more bread in his bag for the first morning break at 9 am. He meets up with his friends and there's some horsing around, jumping on frozen puddles, trying to splash each other as the ice cracks. This at least warms them up, but they have to hurry or they'll be late. They're probably aged eleven or twelve by now and well used to the drudgery that is school. They tramp up to their classroom above the Guildhall – at least the stove is lit which provides some heat – then scramble to their places on the wooden benches, called forms; there are no desks and writing on knees isn't easy, especially with ink which is so messy. Will has just sharpened a new quill, cutting off the feathers at one end and fashioning a pointed nib at the other with his pen-knife.

Thanks be to Jesus and Mary that he has a good memory and can recite quite confidently, especially when they're studying the poet, Ovid, whose stories are his favourites. Some of the boys struggle to memorise the lessons and are always in trouble. Will tries to help the boy who sits next to him who is always being beaten for his failure to learn, but it's not easy with Mr. Jenkins keeping a beady eye on everyone. Today they have to compose a speech in Latin in the style of a famous orator, with all the rhetorical flourishes they can manage: the 'taffeta phrases, silken terms precise, three-pil'd hyperboles'... Will pictures an old guy in a toga, waving his arms around and declaiming loudly to an audience. He enjoys the process of invention, of putting words into his character's mouth. Luckily, his new pen works well and there are few blots.

4. *O This Learning What a Thing it is!*

As the son of a respectable citizen and town councillor, Will was entitled to go for free education to *The King's New Grammar School* in Stratford, which had been established, along with others, by Edward VI in order to raise educational standards across the country. This school still exists in Stratford today and there are a few other remaining grammar schools across England, though the majority disappeared or became comprehensives in the 1970s and 80s. Many of us are unaware of the origins of these schools, though, as the name implies, they were first set up to teach grammar, Latin grammar, along with literature from the classical authors. The curriculum in Will's day was standardised by Royal decree, more evidence of how life under Elizabeth I was tightly controlled.

At that time, children would go to what was called a *petty* school at about four years old to be taught to read and write, though it was not compulsory to go at all. Most girls, if they went at all, usually left by the time they were about six, to be taught at home by their mothers, with the main emphasis being on domestic skills to help them fulfil their likely roles as servants, wives and mothers. This meant that formal education for girls was fairly basic or non-existent unless they were from rich and landed families, when they would have private tutors or governesses at home. The Queen herself loved books and learning and from a young age could read and write Latin, Greek and modern languages like Italian, in addition to her native English.

The town's grammar school had a good reputation and was staffed by masters who were university-educated. Pupils had to be able to read and write before they were admitted at age six or seven. *We have no proof that Will attended this school*, as records of pupils in the 16th century are non-existent, but it's very likely that he did; so much of the knowledge he was later to use in his writing comes from the grammar school curriculum and many of the books, which are known to have influenced him, were regularly used in its teaching.

In *As you Like it*, Will describes a whining schoolboy, *with satchel and shining morning face, creeping like snail unwillingly to school.* Is it any wonder when the syllabus was Latin, Latin and more Latin, with a bit of Christian religious doctrine for good measure? No Science, no modern languages, no Geography, no History, except Roman... no practical, creative, sporting or recreational subjects appeared on the curriculum. I think the polite description would be *intensive*. Latin was the language needed for university or for a career in Law, the Church, teaching or Politics, *ergo* Latin was studied almost exclusively. The classical authors were also considered the epitome of good style and held up as models for schoolboys and university students to imitate. For true culture, too, it was believed that you had to go back to the ancient civilisations of Greece and Rome.

In addition to the unvaried curriculum, school started early, at 6 or 7 am, with a break of two hours for lunch and then a return to study till 5 pm. There were two half days off a week, together with Sunday, and about forty days' holiday a year. Discipline was tough and pupils were beaten with bunches of birch twigs if they misbehaved or got their lessons wrong. Most of their learning was by rote, in other words, exercises had to be memorised perfectly through constant repetition. Of course, some learning today, especially for exams, still relies on good recall of a subject, for example key facts or dates or scientific formulae. Think of a poem you can still remember because you were *made* to learn it by heart, even if you didn't want to! In Will's day, however, there would have been little relief from the mind-numbing monotony of memorising, according to the rigid system devised by Elizabethan educationists.

Fie upon it, fie! as Will might have said. Mind you, he probably didn't loathe school nearly as much as some of the boys, assuming his ability and likely enchantment with the old classical histories and fables, plays and poems, they studied. Then there was his innate susceptibility to words and language; he must have had an intuitive understanding of style, of how words were used for effect, and of what the ancient writers were about with their love of rhetoric, that is the use of persuasive writing or speech. You had to learn all the compositional effects and figures of speech – the rules of rhetoric, in other words. Like lots of skills, you have to learn the rules first before you can think of breaking them to do your own thing, as Will did later. I would guess that at times the schoolboy Will was very bored and lost concentration, afloat on a sea of fancy, but he certainly learnt the rules!

As well as constant writing exercises, the classical education available at the grammar schools probably gave the pupils some opportunities for speaking, declaiming – acting no less – especially in the classes of the more imaginative teachers. So at least the boys could have a go at bringing a speech to life or even enact scenes from Greek or Roman plays. Perhaps this was where Will's first discovered a talent for performance, perhaps he found he could entertain his fellow students and the master in charge, winning hearts and minds, moving them to tears of laughter, joy or sadness. Perhaps there was one teacher who often selected Will to bring a speech alive for the benefit of the class. Sensing the ability of the glover's boy, perhaps he also encouraged Will to write, to use his way with words, to try his own translations or to pen some poetry.

In a nutshell: The 3 R's: Reformation, Royalty & Renaissance

The first R: The Reformation

The reformation of the Christian Church had a huge effect on history, causing a major schism and centuries of sectarian violence. In England and other countries many were to die for being the wrong religion.

In the early 1500s in mainland Europe, a huge religious upheaval started in reaction to Roman Catholicism, the existing Christian church. Martin Luther and many others wanted reform – hence the term Reformation. They sought a simpler kind of Christian worship, with the emphasis on the individual's own conscience and direct relationship with God, without the intervention of the Virgin Mary and all the saints, never mind about the control of priests, cardinals and the Pope, who were seen as being too powerful, too wealthy and too corrupt. *Protesting* against the doctrines of the Church of Rome, members of the new and very different religion became known as *Protestants.* (Possibly with the emphasis on the second syllable originally, though we now stress the first syllable.)

Meanwhile in England, there was an added historical ingredient to go into the mix. Most people know that 1. Henry VIII was a bit of a lad. 2. That he told the Pope to get stuffed, and started his own Protestant branch of Christianity, called (not too imaginatively) the Church of England or Anglicanism. Henry talked a lot of doctrinal guff but it all came down to politics and basic instincts – Henry wanted to divorce his wife and marry Anne Boleyn, hoping for a son, a male heir to the throne. He certainly did not want to be told what to do and not to do by religious leaders.

The new Protestant religion, of which Henry appointed himself Supreme Head, represented huge changes in worship for the people of England. The whole inside of the church building looked different for a start: out went the many painted statues, ornate decoration, stained glass windows, wall paintings and the carved rood screen separating the nave of the church from the chancel, the holy area nearest to the altar. The biggest change in worship was the abolition of the Latin Mass, along with the requirement to confess sins to a priest. *The Book of Common Prayer*, on which Anglican services are still based, was devised and written in English for the new branch of the Christian church and it became the law for an English translation of the Bible to be placed in every parish church.

Another huge change was the deliberate destruction of many monasteries, convents and abbeys; today *the bare ruined choirs where late the sweet birds sang,* as described by Will, can still be seen across the country where once stood the great religious houses. Through his secretary, Thomas Cromwell, Henry took away all power from these establishments, not to mention their enormous wealth which went straight into his own coffers!

After Henry's death, the religious convulsions continued, as his daughter, Mary tried to reinstate the Roman Catholic Church (the Counter-Reformation) and had many Protestants burned at the stake, earning her the title of *Bloody Mary*. She may well have been successful in returning the country to Catholicism, had she lived and reigned longer, and if the next monarch, Elizabeth I, daughter of Henry by Anne Boleyn, had not been firmly Protestant.

Pray or Pay

Will's parents lived through first seismic shifts of the Reformation and the constant religious see-sawing in England. By the time Will was born, the country had veered from being Catholic, then Protestant, then back to Catholicism, then back to Protestantism under Elizabeth, who, as you've heard, kept a tight control on religious matters, making church attendance compulsory and executing subjects for treason if they didn't conform. For those who lived during these turbulent years, security and peace of mind depended very much on whether you could adapt and conform to the current religious situation. Some found the conflict between the state and their private faith or individual conscience impossible to resolve and paid the price with their lives.

On the one hand, the Reformation for many in England, must have represented a relief from the strict oppression of the Roman Catholic Church and many would happily embrace the new forms of worship. On the other hand, the abrupt break with the Church of Rome, the literal and metaphorical iconoclasm, must have brought spiritual dismay and confusion to many brought up in the old religion. Most conformed, but ardent Catholics continued to worship in secret, the politically active risking their lives to try and overthrow Queen Elizabeth.

The second R: Royalty

Most people have seen the much-reproduced picture of King Henry VIII, originally painted by Holbein. Will Shakespeare might have called him the *king of codpieces*: there he stands, an already bulky figure, in aggressive stance, legs apart… tells you all you need to know, really, an example of a picture speaking louder than words.

As an absolute monarch (constitutional monarchy was still way in the future), he had almost complete control over the nobility, parliament and the common people of his land and was soon to control the country's religion, too.

Though Anne Boleyn, for whom he broke with the Church of Rome, never produced a male heir for Henry, eventually, his next wife, Jane Seymour, gave him a longed-for son. Young Edward inherited the throne from his father, but was only to reign for seven years before he died at the age of sixteen. Henry's eldest daughter, Mary, described above, was a devout Catholic like her mother, Katherine of Aragon, and, on ascending the throne, was determined to restore Roman Catholicism to England.

After a short reign, she was succeeded by a Protestant Queen, Elizabeth I, Henry's daughter by Anne Boleyn. In spite of constant threats from Catholic plots, wars and Spanish invasion, events of Elizabeth's reign went from strength to strength, earning her names like *Gloriana* and *Good Queen Bess*. During Will Shakespeare's lifetime, Drake sailed round the world in 1577, and the Spanish Armada was driven back in 1588, among other defining moments which enhanced the Queen's power and the standing of the nation. New colonies were founded through constant voyages of exploration, trade was established and wealth accumulated. England became a country to be reckoned with.

Of all the threats to Elizabeth's long reign from the Spanish, Dutch, Scots and Irish, that from another Queen represented one of the most fearsome. Mary Queen of Scots, a cousin of Elizabeth, increased the Queen's paranoia when she ascended to the throne of Scotland; of course, it was all about religion again. As a Catholic, she was a magnet for plots to kill Elizabeth and make *her* Queen of England instead. Luckily for Elizabeth, Mary was unpopular in Scotland and didn't last long as monarch, but she had a son, whereas Elizabeth was unmarried and childless. When Elizabeth heard of his birth, she is supposed to have cried out despairingly: *The Queen of Scots is lighter of a bonny son and I am of barren stock!*

I'm fascinated by this: if she was really a virgin, how did she know she was barren? Perhaps she was thinking of her father, Henry, and his inability to produce many living children – though he certainly conceived a good number. Perhaps she was just having a broody moment, aware of her biological clock ticking. Whatever the reality of her sex life, Elizabeth, after a succession of suitors, seems to have made a decision not to marry and to have deliberately promoted her virginity in a way that made her an almost semi-divine cult figure. Astute politically and brilliant at what we call PR today, she became a kind of queen-goddess in the eyes of her people.

Perhaps her head didn't always rule her heart in the case of Mary, who was, after all, not only Elizabeth's cousin, but a royal Queen, given divine right by God to rule on earth, a belief held fervently by monarchs and their subjects at the time. Elizabeth had Mary imprisoned for many years before finally signing her death warrant, which it is said, caused her great grief and agonies of conscience. Mary was beheaded in 1587 at Fotheringhay Castle when Will was a young man of twenty-three.

In fact, Mary's son, James VI of Scotland, *did* become the next King of England, in 1603, after Elizabeth's death, thus uniting the two countries: *I will make them one nation, rose and thistle,* he proclaimed, in his enthusiasm for the Treaty of Union, ratified a year later.

Will Shakespeare lived during the reigns of both monarchs, the last of the Tudors and the first Stuart king: the Elizabethan age lasted from 1558 to 1603 and the Jacobean era, under James I, from 1603 till 1625. Both Elizabeth I and James I loved the drama and each played a huge part in helping it to flourish. Will wrote plays for them, visiting their courts with his acting company and performing before them. As his history plays show, he was fascinated by the whole subject of absolute monarchy and the Divine Right of Kings.

The Third R: The Renaissance

The term R*enaissance man*, still used today, usually denotes someone who has wide-ranging talents and interests across different artistic and scientific subjects. Leonardo da Vinci, born in 15th century Italy is probably the best ever example, being a painter, architect, mathematician, engineer, inventor, musician and writer, which, I'm afraid, sets the bar rather high for the rest of us. The Renaissance, itself, which started in Italy, involved a huge revival of interest in the many branches of the Arts and Sciences, a new enthusiasm for learning and an intense appreciation of aesthetic values.

It wasn't that creative achievement and learning hadn't happened before, but a new wave of more passionate pursuit came along at the end of the Middle Ages which continued to affect the cultures of different countries for many centuries after, bringing new thinking and ideas, which proved inspirational. These spread across Europe, helped by the invention of the printing press and the growing number of books becoming available as a result.

There were various other contributory factors, one being the fall of Constantinople (today's Istanbul), and the rescue of books and treasures preserved from Greek and Roman civilisations, which were taken to Italy for safe-keeping. Around these a reverence for classical language and ideals of beauty grew up, so that the Renaissance, in a strange way, looked backwards as well as forwards. As you've seen from the curriculum at Stratford Grammar School, the classical writers were given huge respect, and pupils made to study them.

As well as this inspiration, many of the most talented and creative people who contributed to the Renaissance were also motivated by their strong faith to produce paintings, sculpture, buildings like churches, poetry and music, all to the glory of God. The Renaissance was both sacred and secular in its achievements and its focus on a new way to live, involved spiritual aspiration, so important to nearly everyone in those religious times, but also a new emphasis on the nobility of man, on individuality and the essence of being human, in a way which was excitingly different.

Another factor which helped the Renaissance to flourish involved the rich families in Italy at the time, who were happy to support the new learning financially and become patrons for talented artists, writers and inventors. Theirs was a reflected glory, not to mention fame for their family and posterity. No doubt they shared a sense of making their mark on history, which they certainly did when you think of all the wealth of beautiful buildings, art and artefacts to be seen in Italy.

All of which helps us to understand why the Elizabethans, in general, and Will Shakespeare, in particular, were so obsessed with Italy – from its literature, art and architecture, its spirit of scientific enquiry and its musical composition, to its fashions in clothing: even the enthusiasm for the sport of fencing with rapiers came from Italy. Any Shakespearean actor worth his salt has to learn how to fence convincingly!

The fervour for learning and cultural pursuit had spread across Europe – maybe not so fast as it would today with the Internet and social media – but pretty quickly, arriving in England in the 16th century during the Tudor monarchies. Each country had its own take on the Renaissance: in England, poetry flourished and the new art form, theatre, was born, but there were also painters, like Holbein, architects like Inigo Jones, musicians like William Byrd and Thomas Tallis, along with scientists, inventors, linguists, astronomers, philosophers and many gifted craftsmen. Many of the great houses you can visit today, like Burghley House near Stamford, William Cecil's gift from the Queen, were built and embellished in this period by the nobility and wealthy men who'd been rewarded for services to their monarch and their country.

So England, at the time Will lived, was in the grip of its own Renaissance, celebrating achievement, which led to an increasingly sophisticated society. It was the fashion to learn and to study, to be as accomplished as possible in as many different ways. The printers and booksellers flourished as everyone who could read wanted to buy books. The wealthy started to collect for what were to become valuable libraries in their large town or country houses. New ideas were discussed in the taverns; groups and clubs formed for serious promotion of the many areas of study. Will, himself, may have belonged to some of these, though how he found the time, I don't know: his own knowledge in different fields and subjects is evident in the wide frame of reference throughout his plays. He probably never stopped learning about things which piqued his interest.

5. *In my mind's eye*...What a Falling Off Was There.

A few years later, aged about 13 or 14, a much taller Will is outside the family home in Henley Street. Good-looking, with dark curly hair worn long to his shoulders, his brown eyes seem to look beyond the muddy street with its wood-framed, wattle and daub houses, and over the heads of his younger brothers who run around, kicking a ball. God be blessed that Joan is around to keep them in check: they would vex a saint!.

There's something amiss in the family.

'Thou wouldst not think how ill all's here about my heart!' Will speaks to the air. His parents are inside discussing something of import. By God's blood, why can't they include him in their parley? He's an educated young man now: he has more Latin stuffed in his head, like the bombast used for padding a doublet and hose, than the local lawyer and doctor put together. He knows his father has recently sold several parcels of land, and that he doesn't go to the Corporation meetings or to the church any more, probably to avoid people he owes money to. Will has seen folk whisper behind their hands when he and Joan walk by. At meals they've not had much meat with their vegetables and trenchers of bread for weeks now. One of the sewing maids has left – the new, pretty one who made Will colour up every time he saw her – not the old, fat one who still sits in her corner of the workshop, making jokes about codpieces and their contents. (Knob jokes we'd call them today.) He knows it's only a matter of time before he's taken out of school to help his father with the heavy work of the shop – which he does anyway when needed. A very tempest rages in his brain.

The slippery slope

This last section is just my fancy, but something did go wrong with John Shakespeare's life, something which must have affected the whole family. There was a tipping point when instead of moving onwards and upwards with renewed vigour, playing the part of an honest burgher, a model citizen, he started on a downward trajectory. What does this do to a man, especially one who has built a business and achieved civic office?

We know that as early as 1572 John was involved in some illegal trading of wool. Then he must have got into debt because there is evidence that he sold leases and property, as well as taking out mortgages on his wife's land, her dowry. Maybe he took his eye off the ball, as we would say today, distracted by matters we know nothing of, then straying across the ethical line in business, doing some dodgy deals which sullied his good name? Did he lose custom in the glove shop? There is also some evidence that he was charged with malpractice and usury – money-lending with interest – which always had a bad reputation. Everything started to catch up with him and he received some fines and summonses; his failure to attend church was duly noted. You couldn't hide much in a town like Stratford in Elizabethan England. The dominoes fell, one by one, each knocking the next, and then the next.

As far as we know, John Shakespeare was let off some of his fines, probably because he had served his town so well, but his business went downhill and his reputation suffered. He was no longer a member of the Council, one of the foremost citizens of Stratford: he was now someone who had lost his reputation, stained his good name. From the evidence we have, it seems that he was never to return to his glory days of councillor and successful businessman.

Did he go into a decline? Think of throwing himself off Clopton Bridge? Or was he blessed with resilience in the face of adversity? Did he tough it out or laugh it off? Tweak it by the nose? Snippets of information passed down about John Shakespeare suggest that he was a genial fellow of a cheery disposition, so perhaps he managed to be philosophical about the way Fortune's wheel had turned one way, then the other, for him and his family.

By all the saints...

Another mystery about Will's dad concerns religion and may be relevant here. On at least one occasion, he was charged with *recusancy* – not attending church and taking Holy Communion. Stratford at the time was known as a place where there was considerable resistance to Protestantism and he wasn't alone in being charged. According to evidence found much later, a document hidden in the rafters of the Henley Street house, it seems likely that John was a secret Catholic and still adhered to the old, forbidden form of the Christian worship, with its different doctrines and outlawed practices, together with allegiance to the Pope in Rome as head of the church. If this was the case, it could have been one of the reasons for his troubles, or at least contributed towards them.

Throughout Elizabeth's reign Catholics were not popular at a local level and neighbours sometimes informed against them. On a national level, i.e. by order of the Queen, they were often hunted down, interrogated often under torture, and punished by death, if seen as a threat to the realm. It was forbidden to celebrate Mass, and priests caught doing so would be executed. Some of the fervent Catholic families hid priests in their homes, often in tiny secret rooms called priest-holes, which you can still see today in some of the old country houses. In Warwickshire there were a number of known Catholics, some of them from the Arden family, to whom Will's mother was distantly related.

The Queen tried to appear liberal about religion, famously saying that she didn't want *windows into men's souls* – implying that people's beliefs were private, but the reality was very different. Because of constant fear of treasonous plots to overthrow her, Elizabeth took extreme measures to ensure her safety as queen. Almost alone of all the reigning monarchs of Europe, she was Protestant, keeping the new faith instigated by her father, Henry VIII, the Church of England. This made her very vulnerable indeed, as for example, when Philip, the fervently Catholic King of Spain, sent the famous armada of ships to attack the English.

Even suspicion of being a secret Catholic could go against someone and this could have been what caused John Shakespeare's business to go downhill. Hearsay supports this theory, and it was later claimed that Will's father died a Papist – in other words that he asked one of the Catholic priests in hiding to come and pray for his soul and grant him absolution when he was on his deathbed.

Meanwhile what effect did John's business difficulties have on his family? Everyone who's ever lived in a family – and that's most of us – knows the kind of ripple effects that can result from problems concerning one member but affecting all, causing anything from mild arguments to corrosive feuds that last for generations. Will would have been in his teens, not an easy age at the best of times. He may have lost his respect for his dad, felt resentment and been tempted to judge harshly. Or he may have been saddened, frustrated at not being able to help in spite of all his education. Perhaps he felt mutinous, wanting to flee from the family woes and make something of his life. Whatever his emotional state, it must have been a time of crisis for him and the rest of the family. As well as the financial problems, in 1580 there was a death and a birth in the family: Anne Shakespeare died, aged eight, and the last baby, Edmund, was born later that same year.

Informed guesswork has led scholars to agree that Will must have been taken out of school sometime in the years 1578-80, probably because free education for him was no longer an option after his father's transgressions. He'd have been aged 14 to 16: many of his fellow pupils would have stayed on for another year or two before going into a trade, profession or on to university. No-one knows what Will felt about leaving school or what he did next, but it's generally assumed that he must have helped his father with the family business.

Perhaps this was always the plan, anyway, or maybe John and Mary, proud of their son's literacy, desperately wanted him to do something more suited to his education, professional work like the law or architecture, or at least a clerk's position, penning letters for a living. Overqualified for more menial jobs, their eldest son wasn't yet qualified to do anything else much. Given that the family had lost money and reputation, it wasn't going to be easy. The old adage about *who* you know, not *what* you know was as relevant then as now, probably more so. Methinks Will felt the burden of his education and the expectations of his family.

What is generally accepted, and more or less proved, is that Will *didn't* go to university. There are no records of him attending either Oxford or Cambridge, the only universities of the time in England, or the Inns of Court in London, the training ground for lawyers. Even without John

Shakespeare's loss of income, most fathers in his social position, tradesmen, didn't send their sons to university as they couldn't afford it, though there were exceptions, and there could have been plans to give Will a university education. Years later, when Will eventually arrived in the capital and started to make his way as a writer, he was subject to academic snobbery from some of the university-educated playwrights who looked down on him because he hadn't been to Oxford or Cambridge: they probably thought he hadn't a cat in hell's chance of making it as a writer. The old joke about the University of Life comes to mind here: Will was certainly a student of this educational establishment, as you'll see!

6. The Actors are come hither!

One of the influences on Will's life growing up was almost certainly the crucial one of being able to watch the performances by travelling players who came to Stratford to entertain the townsfolk.

I hope I haven't over-stated my case and made life sound too grim during the early years of Will's life. People have always found reasons to celebrate and enjoy themselves and the Elizabethans were no exception. In fact they were pretty good at it. The rich, who could afford it, made *our* parties today pale into insignificance compared with what they got up to. The Queen herself used to travel from one palace to another for a change of air, literally, because the privies became so blocked that she'd leave them to be sorted out and make for another of her many residences in London. The whole court would go with her and when state business was done, entertainment began, with feasting, drinking, dancing, plays, music, riding, archery and hunting, together with the inevitable flirtations, sexual liaisons and affairs, usually called *debauchery* in Will's time. Then she'd go on visits to noble families who naturally laid on more entertainment for their queen in what was one long party lasting for days. Then the whole circus would move on again and find another venue.

One of Elizabeth's visits was to Kenilworth Castle, just a few miles from Stratford, owned by Robert Dudley, Earl of Leicester, who was one of her favourites, probably her lover. He invited the Queen to stay in 1575 and provided lavish entertainment for her. It's possible that the young Will, aged eleven, was taken to watch the processions of the Queen and nobility as they made their way towards the castle.

Meanwhile the ordinary people had nothing remotely resembling this level of spending and had to content themselves with making the most of what leisure they had from work, especially the public and religious holidays, such as Christmas or the May Day and harvest festivals. There would be dancing and music, eating, drinking and making merry. Across the land in most villages and towns you could find inns, otherwise known as dens of vice, by the Puritans, who disapproved of anything to do with enjoyment. It was true that gambling and prostitution often took place, as well as drinking and the fights which would break out between men who had had too much ale. So what's new? There was also hunting, on a much smaller scale than the organised affairs of royalty and the toffs, and poaching from the rich landowners was pretty common. There were sporting contests on high days and holidays and cruel but popular blood-sports like dog-fighting and cock-fighting. Otherwise, families and friends made their own entertainment, getting together to celebrate occasions like weddings and christenings, enjoying themselves, much as we do today.

But there was some, limited, professional entertainment, too, in the form of travelling actors who visited and put on plays. In fact one of John Shakespeare's jobs as High Bailiff was to supervise these players at the Guildhall in Stratford, where they performed, and to pay them from the civic purse. It's highly likely, then, that Will would have been able to watch their entertainment, probably accompanying his father from an early age. Evidence shows that the actors paid regular visits to Stratford during the time Will was growing up.

This was the *only* professional theatre at the time and even the word, *professional,* should be used pretty loosely. The travelling actors must have varied enormously in talent, from *The Queen's Men* or *Lord Leicester's Men*, to less well-known groups, though none so comically abysmal, we hope, as the amateurs led by Bottom, the weaver, in *A Midsummer Night's Dream* when they tried to perform a play in front of Duke Theseus. The troupes of players travelled the country constantly – a bit like entertainers going on tour today – but for them it was year in, year out, a hard life of being constantly on the road, taking their props and costumes with them. Though they must have brightened up the lives of their audiences no end, theirs wasn't considered a very respectable way of earning a living and in status they weren't much higher than the vagabonds and thieves. This was beginning to change slightly in that wealthy lords started to sponsor them, lending them patronage and some respectability. A troupe of players would then take the name of their patron, as in *Lord Leicester's Men*, and would have some regular work performing for him at his house.

All-singing, all-dancing...

Soon the whole scene was to change again with the advent of the new permanent theatres in London but in the meantime the actors performed at the houses of the rich and, for the ordinary townsfolk, in public places like inn yards, or in the Guildhall in the case of Stratford. They had to be very versatile and there were no clear dividing lines between musicians, actors, acrobats, dancers and so forth. They were all entertainers or players, though many would have their specialist skills. For example, an actor who was a natural comedian would take the comic roles or do some improvised banter with the audience, much as a stand-up comic might do on stage in a club today. Of crucial importance is the fact that *there were no women in the acting companies*, which meant that any female roles in a scene or play were taken by young boys with unbroken voices who were being trained up by the companies of players.

Imagine young Will trotting along with his father to performances at the Guildhall, gazing round-eyed, understanding but not understanding, watching anything from a classical play in translation or a morality play, to a jig or a lewd comic sketch. At school, recitation from the plays of Plautus was a dry thing compared with this, *this real acting*, with wigs, props and costumes, creating an illusion that carried you along with it so that you almost forgot to breathe. As an adolescent with more knowledge of the maelstrom of human emotions, did he thrill to the verse, gripped by the whole *insubstantial pageant* till its dying moments when he came back to four walls, a stage and a group of men bowing low to the appreciative audience in his home town?

How vital were these early experiences of theatre to Will in his formative years? Biographers often seem to underestimate the importance of this early exposure to an art form which, put simply, was to become his life. When still in Stratford he probably saw more theatre than the average child or teenager does today. For him there was only limited access to books in his early years and certainly no cinema, television or electronic games to offer fun and escapism. Did Will become a compulsive follower of the travelling players, watching every performance of his favourite companies, familiar with the scripts and able to repeat them word for word? Did he amuse his friends with renditions of speeches or act out scenes with little embellishments of his own? Did he, growing to early manhood, get to know the actors, chat with them about their lives, join them in the tavern after performances? Perhaps he made contacts that he later used to join one of these professional troupes.

Did he start writing – if he hadn't already – trying out poems or plays, inspired by what he had seen on stage and by what he had already read at school or at home?

In a nutshell: the Rise of Drama in England

There were three main, contributory strands:

1. Classical plays of the Greeks and Romans, comedies and tragedies, which were studied by the educated at school and university.

2. Stories from the Bible which were acted out in church to help people understand them better. Eventually, they spread beyond the church and, known as **mystery or miracle plays**, were acted in street pageants, often on wagons in procession. Some scenes of knockabout (low) comedy were introduced along with the serious content depicting key events from the Christian story. **Morality plays,** also on Christian themes, were written and performed to teach the audience about Good and Evil.

3. Interludes which were short performances enacted between the courses of banquets at the houses of rich noblemen. They often included a court jester character dressed in *motley,* a multi-coloured suit with cap and bells, who would sing, dance, tell jokes or banter with the guests.

All of these elements developed and contributed to what was to become an exciting and much more varied mix of plays written for the new theatres in London, with many playwrights, all vying for fame and fortune. Drama was completely transformed within a few years and the famous period of Elizabethan theatre had begun.

The story of the mid-16th century, paid performers, often called *players* initially, rather than *actors,* is also fascinating. They had formed professional entertainment groups, each employed by a wealthy lord and named after him. Offering a mix of plays, comic sketches, songs, dances, acrobatics and juggling, they also performed for the commoners in public spaces in towns and travelled around the country so that as many people as possible could go and see them.

However, London soon became the focus for performances as more and more plays were written and grew in popularity. To begin with these performances took place, as in other towns, in large public spaces like inn yards and dog-fighting pits, but then – the crucial development – the first playhouses were built in areas like Shoreditch, (Borough of Hackney today): *The Theatre,* [1576], *The Curtain,* [1577], and subsequently on Bankside, (the South Bank) outside the city walls in what is today the Borough of Southwark: *The Rose,*[1587], *The Swan* [1595], *The Globe* [1599] and *The Fortune* [1600]. All of these were modelled on the Greek and Roman arenas and could hold a huge number of people. The name of the first one, *The Theatre,* a Greek work, became the generic term for a building in which plays were performed. Going to watch a play rapidly caught on and became the entertainment everybody wanted to enjoy, though there were no permanent theatres outside the capital city for many years and players continued to travel around the country to perform, as well as appearing in London.

Marriage

ACT TWO:

Marriage and Kids 1582-5

1. An o'er-hasty marriage

Life has a funny way of disregarding your plans at times: wherever you think you might like to go, events overtake you and drag you off down another road. I have more than a shrewd suspicion that what happened next to Will wasn't part of any plan made by him or his parents.

After the record of Will's birth, the next documented evidence of him relates to his marriage and the births of his children. Yes, by God's holy sandals, Will was married with three kids by the time he was 21 – a pretty pass, indeed!

The very first biographer of Will's life, as well as being one of the first editors of his plays, was a man called Nicholas Rowe. Writing in 1709, he says that Will *thought fit to marry while he was very young.* I suspect that Will himself would have appreciated the delicate understatement of the phrase *thought fit,* for which you could substitute the words *was given no choice in the matter* … Will's bride to be was pregnant and it's clear from evidence that friends of her family took legal steps to ensure that Will faced up to his responsibilities. He was only eighteen and still a minor, as the age of majority in those days was 21 – even though the age of consent for a girl was 12 and 14 for a boy.

You've probably heard of the extreme youth of the teenage lovers, Romeo and Juliet. Juliet was almost 14, according to her Nurse, who would have known, having looked after her from birth and breast-fed her as a baby. Romeo was probably older – he talked about sex with his friends, though that's no proof of anything. He was also a good swordsman, as he killed Tybalt, one of the enemy gang... 17 or 18 then? People *did* get married younger in Elizabethan times but not *that* young unless it was for a dynastic alliance in noble or royal families. Juliet's wealthy parents had already got someone lined up for her, the reason why the teenage lovers acted secretly and in haste, with such disastrous consequences. (Spoiler alert!) However, it was usually more common in Elizabethan England for men to marry in their mid-twenties, with women being slightly younger.

With very limited knowledge of human fertility and methods of contraception, extra-marital pregnancies and shot-gun weddings must have happened quite often. However, the legal aspect of marriage at the time was confused by a tradition, still sometimes observed in families, of a betrothal ceremony called *handfasting:* an engaged couple would stand together, hand in hand, and *plight their troth* to one another. *Troth* simply means *truth.* Characters in Will's plays often swear *by my troth*, but here's the thing: this ceremony frequently had the force of marriage, meaning that, after handfasting, couples could live together and have sex. So there must have been quite a few brides who were pregnant when the wedding day came around eventually. In later years handfasting was incorporated into the marriage service making the whole business simpler. The very beautiful words *I plight thee my troth* are still included in some older versions of the Anglican wedding service. At the end of *Twelfth Night*, when Olivia asks Sebastian to *...plight me the full assurance of thy faith/ That my most jealous and doubtful soul/May live at peace,* she is clearly asking for the security of a betrothal ceremony.

We simply don't know whether Will had a *trothplight* with his bride-to-be, Anne Hathaway. Probably not, given the urgency of the situation. One of the mega-mysteries concerning WIll revolves around his marriage and relationship with his wife, Anne, usually referred to by her maiden name and rarely called Anne Shakespeare. So many documents have been lost and the ones we do have only confuse experts, leading to much debate and divided opinion.

Perhaps the air was blue in the Henley Street house with well-known expletives of Anglo-Saxon origin, together with all the current religious ones which were blasphemous, like *Marry* (by Mary), *God's blood* or *'sblood* (*by God's blood*, from where we get *bloody* today) and *Zounds* (*by Christ's wounds*). I've had a bit of fun making up a few of my own in the course of writing this book, as you may have already noticed. Did the Shakespeare parents rant and rave about *unlawful love* and the end of their hopes for their first-born son, who had entangled himself in the age-old way? How could he be so stupid, now we are all undone! Now he'd have to marry the mother of his child? Soon there would be another mouth to feed… yadda yadda.

Whether or not the family were angry, they must have given their permission for him, as a minor, to marry Anne, a local farmer's daughter, who was eight years older than Will (according to the dates on her tombstone). The wedding took place at the end of November 1582 and their baby daughter, Susanna, was born the following May and baptised on the 26th May in *Holy Trinity*, the church by the river, where Will, himself, had been taken for baptism.

2. *In my mind's eye:* Susanna's baptism: Holy Trinity Church 26th May 1583.

Will gazes around the familiar church from his vantage point by the font; he can smell the mix of old dust and tallow candles. The walls have been whitewashed roughly to cover the old paintings depicting heaven and hell but there are still a few of the traditional Catholic doom-scenes across the vaulted ceiling, showing the righteous ascending to sit with God and the sinners being plunged into the flames of hellfire. A salutary lesson for the worshippers and enough to scare the children into behaving for the duration of the Sabbath! A number of stone plinths remain, too, where not long ago had stood gaudy statues of the Virgin Mary and sundry saints, inviting prayer at stations around the church. Idolatry, worshipping graven images, apart from the crucified Christ, that is, has been condemned by the new Protestant state religion.

It's dark and oppressive, where the family all huddle together in the corner by the font: Will feels a creeping despair as the damp walls seem to close in on him. But up in the chancel light floods the stone floor under which the great and the good of Stratford are entitled to be laid. No rood screen divides them from the congregation any more. Will thinks of the dead buried beneath the slabs, of those in the over-crowded graveyard outside and the world-without-end belief they shared in life. He hopes they rest in peace after their labours. Like many, he has a fear of his body being violated after death, his bones dug up and scattered in the charnel house below the church – or worse. He shivers and distracts himself by taking his thoughts outside to the river running free, the effortless swans gliding past banks of new green grass and the darling buds of May, tight-furled in the hedgerows.

Then, with an effort of will, he returns to the scene being enacted before him. He watches his baby daughter in her lace christening cap, like a little bud herself, sleeping in his sister's arms. Joan is so good with babies – always has been – she's had plenty of practice. His mother and father, then Gilbert, the brother next to him in years, and then Anne's brother Richard, complete the circle around the font. He thinks of his wife, back home, pale as her shift after her ordeal. Pray God she is sleeping, to regain her strength. He pictures Anne nursing their baby who turns instinctively, blindly towards the breast, as if her life depends on it – which it does.

Their sixth-month child. A local joke he's grown weary of. The neighbours whisper behind their hands – nothing new there. He's all too aware that he's just given them one more reason for them to gossip about his family. Can the once respected name of Shakespeare plummet any lower?

The vicar, Henry Haycroft – lovely, alliterative name – gently takes the baby from Joan and, holding her with practised skill in the crook of his left arm, makes the sign of the cross over her. In the name of the Father... he intones (et filii et spiritus sancti, they used to say) and holds her out over the water in the font. Her eyes snap open as she senses her vulnerability, the air beneath her, but she doesn't cry out as he splashes the water on her forehead. Will feels proud. Sweet Susanna, he thinks, flesh of my flesh, blood of my blood. My sweet little Susanna!

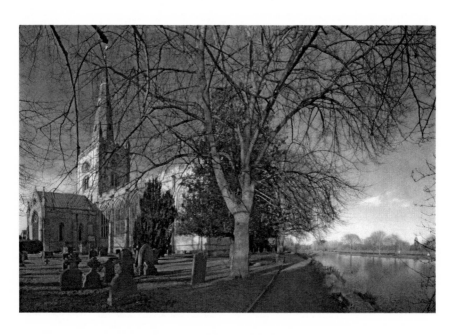

Holy Trinity Church, Stratford-upon Avon.

3. Anne hath her way

Meanwhile what of Will's wife? What part did she play in all this – apart from the obvious? Did her heart leap up or lurch with the secret knowledge that she was to bear a child? Did she love her child's father and long to be wed to him? Was she happy to leave her brother and his family at the old farmhouse in Shottery and move to the crowded Henley Street home as the wife of William Shakespeare?

Poor Anne – in most biographies she's a shadowy figure at the best of times and, at worst, she's depicted as a predatory female who trapped Will into marriage, being eight years older and desperate for a husband. Maybe she was the more sexually experienced of the two and led him astray in a field at haymaking time? According to the double standard which still exists today, the woman is often seen as a bit of a slut, while the man is just a lad, proving his macho credentials.

As if this isn't bad enough, Anne is often given the reputation of being something of a shrew – Will wrote a play called *The Taming of the Shrew*, after all, so there's the proof! Add to this the incontrovertible fact that he left her behind in Stratford and went to live in London for most of his life, so he must have wanted to get away from her, *ergo*, she was a nagging wife…

You don't have to be a feminist to turn this argument on its head; looked at the other way, you could make a very good case for Will being the seducer, meeting Anne one summer and making hay while the sun shone. Autumn and responsibility came soon enough for Anne and Will. Only a few years later, he turned his back on family duties and headed for the theatres of London! You don't need a Law degree to make a good case against *Sweet William*, as Anne might have called him. But usually Anne seems to be the culpable one – after all, it could look as if she just stayed home, spent the money he sent back from London and took little interest in how he earned it. In this way the myth of the unhappy marriage has gained credence over the years. Nowadays biography is more realistic, but, we have no hard evidence either way, apart from the knowledge that Will moved to London and spent his working life there. We don't even know for certain that Anne *didn't* go with him, but, as Will lived in fairly simple lodgings most of the time, with no room for a wife and kids, experts have reached the inevitable conclusion that Anne Shakespeare spent most of her life in Stratford, raising Will's children, being what today would be called a single parent.

Against his will?

In *A Midsummer Night's Dream*, there is a discussion about how the course of true love never runs smooth. Whether Anne and Will were *misgraffed* (unsuitably matched) in respect of their age gap, or *misgraffed* for any other reason, we'll never know. Perhaps they were well-suited and happy, as Carole Ann Duffy, the current Poet Laureate, suggests: in her poem *Anne Hathaway*, she imagines Anne's thoughts after Will's death, taking the controversial view that theirs was a wonderfully passionate relationship and not an enforced union:

The bed we loved in was a spinning world

Of forests, castles, torchlight, cliff-tops, seas

Where he would dive for pearls.

If only Anne or Will had kept a diary – or written some love letters. Maybe they did but none have been found. Their story happened four and a half centuries ago. We have no idea how they met, but Anne's home was only a mile away so it's probable that the two families knew each other, if only through business, perhaps the buying of wool, animal skins or corn. Young people will always find a way of being together if there is a fizz of attraction between them, a fever in the blood.

From the rather mysterious and conflicting evidence relating to their marriage, it seems unlikely that they had any kind of arranged courtship or betrothal, approved by their two families; there wasn't enough time. Once the families found out about Anne's pregnancy, they set about arranging the wedding, but here's the rub! It didn't take place in Stratford, nor in

Shottery, Anne's home village. A special licence was applied for in the court at Worcester, some miles from Stratford, so that Anne and Will could, it seems, marry quickly away from their own parishes. In addition, two men, friends of the Hathaways, bought a bond, a very expensive legal document, to ensure the wedding went ahead. This was **not** common practice: methinks Anne's relatives were making very sure that Will turned up for the ceremony. From the surviving paperwork, it looks as if the couple were wed at the very end of November, before the Christmas season when marriages weren't allowed. And before the reason for their haste was visible to all.

The marriage bond is the only document to survive, along with a register recording the application for the marriage licence – and both contain some very odd details. Apart from the usual careful legal language, the names seem to have been filled in without any care whatsoever.

On the bond is Anne Hathaway's name and Will is called William *Shagspere*, one of many different versions of his name, but, to my mind, the most humorous, given the circumstances. The register, however, gives a seemingly *different* woman as Will's intended – someone called *Anne Whately*. Researchers have understandably been bewildered by this confusion: how many women was Will planning to marry, by God's holy fingernails! The explanation usually given is that the clerk made an error and put *Whately* instead of *Hathaway*! Was he drunk? Dyslexic? In need of eye-glasses? The names aren't at all similar. Some Shakespeare scholars *do* believe that Will was intending to marry one Anne – perhaps one he loved dearly – and ended up having to marry the other one because she was pregnant! It *would* explain the complicated measures taken to get Will and Anne Hathaway hitched at all costs, secretly, away from home.

No-one has been able to find a girl called Anne Whately, though the surname is a local one to Stratford; no-one has managed to find an even half-way satisfactory explanation for the anomalies of the marriage document, adding to the frustration, but leaving you free to revitalise the relationship between Anne and Will Shakespeare in whatever way you wish.

The Victorian Spin

I recently came across a facsimile of a Victorian painting in an early edition of Will's plays, entitled *The Courtship of William Shakespeare*. I'll describe it: a young lad (Will), with dark hair curling on his beautifully clean collar, sits beside a young woman, (Anne), on a separate chair, holding her hand most decorously. She has her head bowed modestly over a book on her lap. The light from the window above illuminates her delicate features, her maidenly blush, and her hair tucked tidily into a snow-white cap. Both young people look shy, as if totally innocent of the world and its ways .... You get the picture! It was definitely airbrushed! The Victorians wanted to present Will in the best possible light (sic), so the wooing of Anne Hathaway is portrayed here as very formal and proper, with no hint of indelicacy, let alone lustful looks leading to at least one tumble in the hay, followed by a highly litigious shot-gun wedding. Thus, the reasons for the marriage were probably hushed up for years and the image of the Immortal Bard kept pure and perfect. Nowadays we sex up everything but the Victorians were experts at doing the opposite; sexing-down!

Incidentally, it was George Bernard Shaw, the early 20th century playwright, who coined the humorous term *bardolatry*, to describe the almost fanatical Shakespeare worship of his time whereby the national icon could do no wrong! He was having a bit of a pop at Will and the whole Shakespeare industry, as you've probably guessed, but the Bard, who did so much for the English language himself, would no doubt have approved of Shaw's coinage of such a witty, new term.

So whatever spin you put on it, Will took the path of marriage, children and domesticity very early on. I can't imagine his parents being altogether pleased at the turn events had taken for their educated eldest son. We know that they had a large family of their own and were perhaps already looking to Will to earn some money or to help their failing business. Will had a baby brother, Edmund, who was only two years old. And now he was about to become a father himself.

Most researchers assume that, though Anne had some money of her own from her deceased parents, she and Will lived with the Shakespeare family in Henley Street. If Will's father had any other plans for his son at this time, they were no doubt shelved and the extended family of eight, shortly to become nine, then eleven, lived together in one household.

Susanna was probably rocked to sleep in the same cradle which was used for Will and his siblings. Anne soon became pregnant again and in 1585 gave birth to twins, named Judith and Hamnet, after friends of the family, the Sadlers, who lived nearby. Following the births of all the children, Anne would have been *churched*, the Christian custom for the mother to go to church for blessing after childbirth, even if the child was stillborn or died in the first few weeks of life. Whatever the neighbours whispered about the young couple, Anne's reputation was probably not enhanced by the contemporary belief that a woman who gave birth to twins must be a bit of a nymphomaniac!

4. Early love poem

One of Will's sonnets – short love poems, which he probably wrote on and off throughout his life – fascinates biographers looking for links between his writing and his life. In the absence of letters to Anne, it's the next best thing and is probably one of the earliest examples of Will's poetry, if not *the* earliest. Not published until 1609 with the collection of other sonnets, it seems to contain a pun on the name Hathaway, right at the end. The Elizabethans were obsessed with puns, by the way, and liked to include little verbal jokes, like cryptic clues or secret messages, in their poetry. Some were intriguingly clever; others were a bit cheesy, like tabloid newspaper headlines today.

I'll quote the whole poem, then you can make up your own mind – or skip this section, if you prefer. The writer, young Will, speaks of the pain of love, his *woeful state,* and the fact that the woman he loves rejected him initially. Not to put too fine a point on it, she *hated* him. However, she changed her mind about him and *threw hate away – Hathaway* – geddit? I know it sounds a bit contrived but if Will wrote it when only eighteen it's not a bad effort. It's possible, too, that Hathaway was pronounced Hattaway in the Warwickshire dialect. We don't know how lots of words were pronounced in those days, including Will's own surname. Will concludes the poem dramatically, by saying how she, the woman, *saved his life* by returning his love.

It's the only poem written by Will that mentions his wife – if it does. Was it just a case of conventional sentiment, the poet playing the part of the spurned lover (a fashionable stance) and trying out the new verse form from Italy? Or does it convey genuine feeling, especially gratitude, towards Anne for loving him, revealing the depth of their early relationship? I would like to believe the second option, but then I'm a bit of a romantic.

Those lips that love's own hand did make

Breath'd forth the sound that said 'I hate',

To me that languish'd for her sake;

But when she saw my woeful state,

Straight in her heart did mercy come.

Chiding that tongue, that ever sweet

Was used in giving gentle doom;

And taught it thus anew to great;

'I hate' she altered with an end

That followed it as gentle day

Doth follow night, who like a fiend

From heaven to hell is flown away.

'I hate' away from hate she threw,

And saved my life, saying 'Not you.'

Statue of William Shakespeare in Central Park, New York.

The Journey

ACT THREE:

The Road to London

1. *In my mind's eye*: The Journey

In the rain the horses of the five men plod slowly along the muddy track which is the main road from Stratford to Oxford. The leading rider, Will Greenaway, a carrier of goods between Stratford and London, is used to hard journeys and bad weather, as his tanned leather-look complexion proclaims. As well as carrying a pack full of parcels and saddle bags stuffed with papers, he often escorts other travellers because there's safety in numbers. So far this day's ride has been uneventful: his sword has stayed in the belt around his waist.

As they reach the crest of the hill, he points to the horizon where the spires and cloud-capped towers of Oxford shimmer through the wet mist. The slow-gaited horses are happy to pick up their pace and trot on in hope of journey's end.

The youngest of the travellers is in his early twenties, with brown eyes and dark hair, plastered back from his high forehead by the incessant rain, in spite of the large brimmed hat he wears. Will Shakespeare, for it is he, looks up in anticipation. His mind has been back home for most of this tedious, wet journey: he thinks of the crowded house in Henley Street, of Anne, his wife who will be helping his mother to prepare the supper, of his sturdy little daughter, of his baby twins, now weaned, lying like starfish on a blanket beach. They all seem to be receding further and further, as if they're moving and not him. He thinks of the lush green water meadows, the swans on the river and the sweet sorrow of parting.

His companions are looking brighter at the thought of food and hot ale, of the warm fireside at The Crown tavern and then blessed sleep, even if they have to share beds with the fleas in the straw. Will, too, feels his spirits lift, the resolve strengthen within him. Is the new act of his life's drama about to unfold?

2. The Gap Years

This William, being inclined naturally to poetry and acting, came to London, I guess about eighteen, and was an actor.

These are the rather spare, colourless words of Will's first biographer, Nicholas Rowe, written in 1709, ninety-three years after the dramatist's death. The clue is in the word *guess*: as with all biographers since, he's had to go in for a bit of deduction – *he didn't really know.*

Except for the names of the Stratford carrier and the tavern, where Will was to stay regularly on his three-day journeys between London and Stratford, I have imagined the day that he rode towards Oxford in the rain. I am haunted by the thought of that first journey when Will left home, on the edge of the unknown. Did he have a sense of something momentous about to happen? Did he feel an excitement that he was finally about to make something of his life? Or did the rain add to his despair, and the weight of the world upon his shoulders?

Or perhaps the scenario was somewhat different and he travelled with another group of people, a company of actors on foot, maybe *The Queen's Men* who were a man short after one of their number had died in a brawl that got out of hand. They'd take turns at pulling their handcart, full of props and costumes. Instead of the inn's shelter, Will might have slept in barns and hedgerows. Perhaps the sun was shining and the apprentice actor would join in with the laughing and joking of his new friends, feeling free from the confines of home, where he could do nothing right.

Perhaps there'd been an almighty row, a challenge, a gauntlet thrown down by his father. An appropriate metaphor for a seller of gloves. *See if you can make a living with those vagabonds, then! That's all you think about, acting, and writing poetry,* and *getting wenches with child!*

Whatever happened, one thing is sure – that the course of Will's life was altered for ever by his decision to go to London.

Making Waves

But we don't know the date of this memorable journey. After the birth of Will's twins, nothing is known of his life for the next seven years, often known as *the lost years,* until a famous reference to him in 1592 places him in London and makes it clear that he has arrived, in both senses of the word, and started on the road to fame as a writer of plays. How on earth he did this is the biggest mystery of all those surrounding Will Shakespeare. What did he do in the intervening, *low-res* wilderness years? The Will conundrums multiply at this most crucial stage of his life: *when* and *why* did he go to London?

Young Will, at twenty-one, seemed to be severely restricted by duties, domesticity and dependants. Remember, by *dependants,* you can include, not only Anne and the children, but all his younger siblings, together with his parents who were not thriving as they had formerly. They may well have looked to him for a solution to their financial problems, which could have been the reason he went off to London. Did he go with their blessing or did he simply take off without their consent? Did he jump or was he pushed?

It's possible that he left Stratford to go some somewhere else first: researchers have suggested all sorts of locations, ranging from the North of England to Holland to Italy – even a voyage across the Atlantic has been proposed – but no-one knows for sure. There is some very plausible but not quite conclusive evidence which suggests that Will may have gone to a house near Blackburn in Lancashire, as a tutor to the Catholic de Hoghton family. He probably did some acting while there to entertain the family and possibly met up with a group of players who would prove useful contacts. It's always assumed that he left Stratford sometime after the birth of the twins in1585. Legend has it that he got into trouble poaching deer from local landowner, Sir Thomas Lucy, and had to disappear quickly. As researchers have found that Sir Thomas didn't, in fact *have* a deer park, at the time, this theory would seem to be a bit of romantic folklore of the Robin Hood-stealing-from-the-rich variety! Perhaps the Shakespeare family invented it to hide the fact that Will had left Stratford under a cloud, or even as a cover story to conceal more serious trouble. Theories about the family's Catholicism are popular at the moment, so maybe Will was in some kind of real danger linked to his family's religion and had to flee his home.

It's unlikely that anyone will ever discover the truth now, or manage to prove conclusively why Will left home, but the main options are best summarised as follows:

- Will wanted to be a writer and decided to head for London where plays were becoming very popular, and where there were wealthy patrons to encourage aspiring playwrights and poets.

- He was seduced by the theatre and wanted to act. He had become passionate about the entertainments staged by the travelling players who frequently visited Stratford and decided to join one of the companies.

- He left to do something else first: perhaps became a soldier or sailor or, more likely, started a profession like law or teaching, for which his education would have qualified him. Possibly he became a tutor to a wealthy family in Lancashire, a Catholic stronghold at the time, where, if, indeed, he *had* fled for religious reasons, he would be among friends.

- He needed to get away from an increasingly unhappy marriage.

- He left to restore the family fortunes as his father was seriously in debt.

- He *had* to leave because he was in trouble, whether with Sir Thomas Lucy, whom he's supposed to have lampooned in mocking verses, or with the authorities, always suspicious of Catholic subversion.

As with many mysteries about Will, it's possible to argue from totally opposing positions. The dichotomy of the Bard's life has been a growing fascination for me in the research and writing of this book. Either Will acted alone, taking a giant step into the unknown, not knowing where it would lead, **or** the family were involved, initially, at least, arranging some kind of employment away from home through someone they knew. Whatever the truth, I think it's most unlikely, that they would have chosen the very insecure and low status job of a travelling player for him, or even wanted him to join a company of London actors. Both would have been considered very strange choices at the time, beneath him educationally and socially. The new form of entertainment, the theatre, was becoming more professional by the day, but anyone connected with it was still seen as being morally dubious. Surely Will's parents would have wanted something more steady and respectable for their first born son?

Whatever you think happened, you can be fairly sure that Will's leaving home was a decisive moment, the end of something and a new beginning. Whatever the truth, he and Anne were destined to spend most of their married life apart, though they didn't know it at the time. On the one hand, with all the models for different relationships today, most couples still choose to live together and are thought odd if they don't. On the other hand, out of financial necessity, men throughout the ages have had to leave home in search of work. It's known that Will returned to Stratford regularly, and continued to support his family throughout the twenty or so years that he was in London. It was a three-day journey on horse-back so, when his career was flourishing, he probably only managed to travel home once or twice a year at most. Whatever his reasons for leaving, he must have missed his home town and the countryside around – at least at first – and have pictured the family going about their familiar routines. Perhaps they were always the mainstay of his life.

Did he feel liberated from the ties of his marriage or did he miss Anne, longing for her in the London nights when it was bitter cold in winter, or stifling hot in summer? Did he lie awake, listening to the snores, creaks and groans of the other lodgers, or the sound of a brawl outside in the street? Did he think of his children asleep and dreaming their innocent dreams? He must have become used to leading a kind of double life – free but not free, single but married, a Protestant but a secret Catholic. A father but mainly an absent one. And what of Anne? Did she resent her husband's freedom, when she was the one feeding and caring for their children, tucking them up in bed, telling them stories to keep him present in their thoughts? Did she envy his double life – and feel that she was leading only half a life without him?

Whatever you think – and I've reflected on this hugely significant turning point a lot – if Will had stayed in Stratford as a dutiful husband and father, it's highly unlikely he'd have ever written his famous plays. Even if Anne and the family had followed him to London to live, you wonder whether his output would have been as great or as varied. The lifestyle of a single man, essentially the way he lived in London, was undoubtedly the key to Will's creativity and to his success. The sheer volume of work he produced is unbelievable: just from a practical standpoint, how would he have found the time to write if he'd been going home each day to his wife and children?

This isn't the same as saying he was better off without them: he never entirely deserted his family back home. It's more than possible, as I've suggested, that the Stratford half of his life gave him stability; certainly his rural background and experiences growing up in Stratford were an essential part of who and what he was, and vital to his development as a writer.

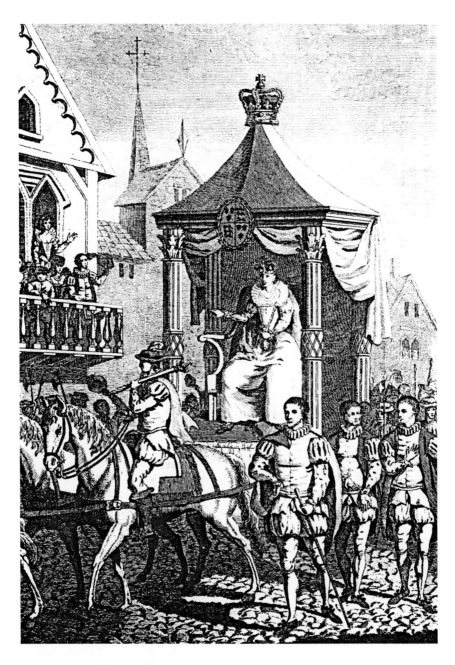

Queen Elizabeth I in procession through the streets.

3. The City c.1592.

Going to London must have been a huge culture shock for Will, a country bumpkin who'd spent the first part of his life in a provincial, market town; he'd probably never been there before though he could have done some sort of business trip with his father, you never know. Like many before and after him, he probably felt charged with the excitement of arriving in the capital and gradually becoming part of the city where so much was happening and everything was constantly changing.

With a population of 200,000, London wasn't nearly as big as it is now, most of it being contained by walls within the area we now call the *City*. Even so, everything would be bigger, busier, noisier, even smellier than Stratford. People, animals, and carts would throng the narrow streets where mediaeval buildings almost met each other across the street, at the higher levels. If you looked up, you realised that they were often three, four, even five storeys high, almost shutting out the view of the sky. But most of the time you had to keep your eyes down to avoid the piles of rubbish in the streets and the streams of ordure flowing over the cobbles. There would, however, have been some pleasant fragrances, as people planted their gardens with flowers and sweet-smelling herbs, both of which could be picked and strewed on floors of their houses or even crushed into clothes to help personal hygiene.

The wooden 'O'

The buildings included hovels, grand merchants' houses, inns, shops, churches, palaces and – most relevant for Will – the new, permanent theatres, the first to be built expressly for the performance of plays. These were often fairly crudely constructed, in an octagonal shape, with their steep sides of wattle and daub and tiers of wooden seating which were sheltered by a thatched roof to afford some protection from the weather for the more highly priced seats. At the back of the stage was a tall, thin building, also thatched, which included the *tiring house* where the actors changed. There were doors for their entrances to left and right, and a small room for interior scenes like banquets and so on, but most of the performance took place on the huge apron stage which projected out into the arena, open to the elements. The *groundlings*, the poorest people, who paid a penny for their tickets, *stood* around the stage to watch the play. Trumpets would sound and a flag would be flown from the roof when a performance was about to start.

There was a balcony *above* the stage, used for scenes like the famous love scene in *Romeo and Juliet*, and a trapdoor built *into* the stage for underground appearances and disappearances, like the spooky night visitation of the ghost of Hamlet's father. There was no lighting so the darkness on the battlements at Elsinore would be described by a character in the play. Likewise, there was little scenery of the sort we often use today – perhaps sometimes a painted backdrop, but that was all. Again it was the writer's job to describe the imaginary surroundings so the audience could picture the scene in their mind's eye. A few items of furniture and some props would add realism, together with costumes, which were often rejects from the wardrobes of the wealthy.

Depending on when Will arrived in London, there were only two or three theatres in existence, all in the Shoreditch area, but soon more were to be built across the river in the area known as Bankside, outside the city walls. The first, *The Theatre*, was the brainchild of James Burbage, a shrewd man who could spot a business opportunity at fifty paces across a rat-infested slum. More later about his son, Richard, who was to become a famous actor, definitely an A-lister, and one of Will's closest colleagues and friends. Some similar-looking arenas and buildings were not theatres at all but bear-baiting and dog-fighting pits, built on the same circular arena model and just as popular for recreation with the bloodthirsty Elizabethans, who could choose between a tragedy or some animal cruelty, depending on their mood, with some serious drinking as a part of the entertainment on either occasion...

Indeed, another businessman, called Philip Henslowe, was one of the first entrepreneurs in what you might call the *pleasure and leisure* business: he owned theatres, fighting arenas and brothels, and clearly didn't mind mixing it up so long as his different venues made money. Which they did. He may have been a bit of a shady character, but his notes and book-keeping were meticulous and it's from his paperwork that such a lot of accurate information has been gleaned about the beginnings of professional theatre in England, the way the theatres were managed and which of Shakespeare's plays were performed in the early part of his career.

A Paradox

Most capital cities today contain extremes of wealth and poverty, representing a melting pot of all the good and bad in teeming humanity. Elizabethan London was no exception. In fact it probably proved the rule more than almost any other city at that time! And it was growing fast, beginning to spread beyond its boundary walls, what with all the visitors, immigrants and people, like Will, who had come to the city to find opportunities for work, trying to make something of their lives. Even so, it was still much easier, than in today's urban sprawl, to leave London, by road or river, and be immediately in the countryside around.

In the sixteenth century, the River Thames is the lifeblood of the city and a symbol of all that is both grand and far from grand. Everyone travels by river, from the poorest, in the hired tilt-boats, to the Queen, moving between her various palaces in the Royal Barge. Elegant buildings line the river but there are also slum areas where crime and violence are rife. There are no embankments so the river floods regularly, and sometimes in the severest of winters it freezes over. It is both waterway and water-source, not to mention a sewer as well.

The Elizabethans have built only one bridge across the Thames, London Bridge, which has all sorts of shops and houses perched atop and is always thronged with people. It is also here that the decaying and decapitated heads of the recently executed are displayed on spikes, to demonstrate the fate of those who commit crimes against Queen and country. The Tower of London stands close by, one of many grim prisons for offenders, whose method of execution – if sentenced to death – usually depends on their social standing. Nobility and royalty are beheaded within the precincts on Tower Green, the fate of two of Henry VIII's wives. Lesser mortals are brought out and dragged on a hurdle through the streets to be hanged in a designated public place, like Tyburn, as a deterrent to others. Their deaths are watched by huge crowds who gather for executions, which are stage-managed like dramatic performances, with the condemned being given the opportunity to say some last words to the spectators. The most gruesome and barbaric method of capital punishment involves the victims being hanged, drawn and quartered – cut down from the scaffold when still alive, then castrated and their entrails removed from their stomachs to be burnt in front of them. Finally, their bodies are quartered, i.e. hacked into four pieces. Watching a public execution, especially one involving such butchery as this, is highly popular.

No less cruel was burning at the stake, particularly favoured by the previous Queen, Mary, for Protestants who refused to swear allegiance to her Roman Catholic faith, and, before that, employed by her father, Henry VIII, for priests and Catholics who refused acknowledge *him* as the head of the church in England. To many of us in more secular times, it's hard to comprehend the significance of doctrinal differences in one faith and how such cruelty can be carried out in the name of religion, but, of course, it still goes on.

Violence is, indeed, the backcloth to much that happens in London in the 16th century, and yet, paradoxically, other aspects of life are civilised, sophisticated and aspirational, showing mankind in his quest for beauty, knowledge and enlightenment. Centuries later the poet Tennyson was to refer to *the spacious times of great Elizabeth,* whose subjects were influenced throughout the Renaissance, by the emotional impact of Art and the thirst for scientific understanding of the physical world. In his phrase, Tennyson implies the sheer boundlessness of intellectual curiosity at the time: literacy was rising, and down at the market by St Paul's you could choose from a vast selection of books coming into print all the time, as more of the population learnt to read and wanted to read to learn. Perhaps Tennyson was also suggesting the literal expansion of the Elizabethan world through travel and exploration. Today, through technology, our world is shrinking, the exact opposite: you can go anywhere on Google Earth at the click of a button. Imagine living in an age when your world view was changing and widening constantly, as new lands across the seas were found and charted for the first time.

But – and it's a big *but* – the other side of Elizabethan progress is a callous lack of concern for human suffering, setting a low value on life, which we find appalling today. As Charles Dickens said about a different city and another age, *It was the best of times, it was the worst of times... it was the season of Light, it was the season of Darkness.*

Money talked, as it does today, and the *spacious times of great Elizabeth* certainly allowed for entrepreneurship and climbing the social ladder. You could seek your fortune in the towns, especially London, and England was becoming a much richer country; a growing middle class was gaining affluence and the old feudal hierarchies were beginning to break down, though there was still a massive chasm between rich and poor. Merchants were trading abroad, soldiers and sailors could lead lives of adventure and, most famous of all, explorers, like Drake and Raleigh, were bringing back goods and wealth from abroad, often from ships they had plundered in sea battles.

Will Shakespeare was living in an era of transition and, as luck would have it, had elected to go to London at the most crucial time for the incredible new developments in drama, and its showcase, the new, professional theatre.

4. Making Waves

By1592, Will had arrived on the scene – an appropriate expression for someone joining a theatre company. He must have gone through his own self-imposed and very hard-working apprenticeship, learning to act and beginning to write plays. He probably started at the bottom and, according to some accounts, he may even have looked after horses outside the theatres while their owners were inside. But, perhaps for the first time in his life, it was his own choice. He was doing what *he* wanted to do.

What his initial steps were, can only be imagined and guessed at, but evidence has survived to show that, whether he crept or leapt to fame, he was well known enough in 1592, when he was twenty-eight, to provoke some jealous remarks from a writer who clearly resented him. This was Robert Greene, a university man, who was dying in poverty at the time and, probably bitter at his own failure, called Will, the outsider, *an upstart crow*. There's no doubt that he's referring to Will, because he makes a pun on his name, referring to him as *Shakescene*, a player and a Jack-of-all-Trades, in other words implying that he's not a serious playwright because he does a bit of everything!

Greene wasn't far wrong with the Jack-of-all-Trades insult. They say no publicity is bad and these un-subtle barbs tell us something of the unusual way Will had broken into the theatre world as actor and playwright – not to mention horse-holder. There was no precedent for an intelligent provincial youth with an incomplete grammar school education to take on the *university wits* and beat them at their own game, but Will had clearly done just that. Even today there are people who, out of academic snobbery, can't or won't believe that Will's plays were written by him and will go to amazing lengths to try and prove that someone else wrote them. But you could also argue, as Shakespeare scholar, Jonathan Bate, does, that Will probably wouldn't have written his plays if he'd been to university and become absorbed in the world of academe, losing the common touch and lacking the regular contact with the London theatre scene.

Most of us enjoy hearing a success story of someone who's triumphed against the odds, and want to share the feel-good factor; the more humble the beginnings, the more obstacles in the way, the better! Think famous scientists and inventors, successful businessmen and entrepreneurs, explorers, freedom fighters, sportsmen and women, artists and writers, and, above all, the stars of stage and screen today. Think of the appeal of talent shows like *The X factor* and reality shows like *The Apprentice*; everyone loves a winner! Unless you're a rival, of course.

Poor old Greene! After his death, the printer published an apology to Will – an indication that Will was already respected and that many felt the criticism unjustified.

There were no talent shows in Will's time and no Susan-Boyle-moment, but there must have been high points you can only imagine: for example, the first time Will acted a part of more than a few lines on stage, or the first time he heard the words from his own pen declaimed before a huge London audience... Perhaps there were gales of laughter at a comic scene he'd written, or the spectators were moved to tears by a speech of pathos. There would be performances of plays in which he'd collaborated, co-writing plays being common throughout this period of drama. Then the first performance of a play that was all his own work. By 1592, it's thought that Will had written and seen performed as many as five or six of his own plays, though experts fail to agree on exactly which ones and their chronological order.

Did Will sense his power to hold those crowds of two-to-three-thousand in the palm of his hand? Did he relish the hush of their held breath before the thunder-clap of applause engulfed the galleries and reached all the actors, including him, taking their bows on stage?

All in a day's work

If you'd previously thought of Will Shakespeare as an elderly, bearded literary dude, writing at leisure in an elegant oak-panelled room – you were wrong. If you imagined him sitting in a garret, working away to make his name – you were closer, but only half right. Much of his writing must have been done when he was alone in the wee small hours, but Will was no solitary creative genius in the day. He was part of a team, a fully involved member of a group of actors, finding his feet and learning the ropes.

On his arrival in London, Will may have headed for the theatre area of Shoreditch, organising lodgings or staying with friends, like Richard Field, a friend from Stratford, who was apprenticed to a printer. He probably did have to start at the bottom, being a general dogsbody with one of the companies, maybe through contacts from Stratford days, such as the actors he already knew from visits to the Guildhall. Working backstage, selling tickets, testing actors on their lines, taking walk-on parts, copying scripts, amending scripts... one thing you can bet on is that Will did it all and was a fast learner in his new environment.

No-one really knows how good an actor he became: obviously his writing took over, though not exclusively, as he continued to act smaller roles for many years. Given his understanding of human nature, it's likely that he could act well, feeling his way into a part, able to convey the enhanced emotions of drama. Actors at the time, especially those with main roles, had to have phenomenal memories, as there was often a different play performed every day, unlike today where one play or show will often run for weeks or months at a time. The Elizabethan players had to provide variety, or go under – and there was increasing rivalry between the different acting companies. You needed energy and stamina if you were involved in the theatre in any way. A new form of entertainment had arrived, rather like the coming of the cinema or television in the 20th century, and the people went mad for it. Great actors could become stars, entrepreneurs had new opportunities to open theatres, and, above all, talented writers were needed to provide plays, the dramatic raw material. As the theatre exploded into life, many plays were to be written during the next two decades, though not all good ones, of course. There were growing numbers of aspiring playwrights.

At the start, for Will, it must have been full-on, all day, every day, a total immersion in the life of the theatre. We assume a schedule of rehearsals in the mornings, with a build-up to the performance in the afternoon, trumpets sounding to summon everyone to the theatre. Without lighting, evening performances weren't possible, except by candle-light at court and in wealthy houses, so plays for the public were usually put on in the afternoons in broad daylight. At least there would be time for the company to relax and let off steam in the local tavern by nightfall; but the next day the whole process would start all over again. And soon Will would have to find time for writing, too! He must have been insanely busy.

Will must have had the self-belief that he could be one of the new writers, who could tap into the new enthusiasm for theatre, giving the public what they wanted. He must have dreamed of rave reviews. No-one knew, of course, how this popular craze would pan out, nor how long it would last. But Will had arrived at just the right time and methinks would have sensed it in the air around him, relying on his own strong intuition. Only history would prove just how good his timing was and how auspicious his move to London in the closing decades of the sixteenth century.

5. The play's the thing...

The question of popular appeal was vital. Some writers had it and some hadn't. It was as simple as that – and still is today.

One of the most extraordinary aspects of Elizabethan drama was that it appealed to people of all classes and all levels of education. It was supported by the Queen and nobility, without whom it wouldn't have flourished. The well-to-do went to see plays; so did the lawyers and university students, the merchants and the tradesmen, soldiers, sailors, foreign visitors to London, servants, apprentices and lowly labourers. The writers' target audience was a dauntingly wide one, no doubt about that. Never again in the history of drama did so many people from so many walks of life go to the theatre.

They piled into the new purpose-built arenas, which could hold up to 3,000 people, either seated in the galleries or standing, for a penny, in the area around the massive stage. Experts on Elizabethan drama often suggest that the atmosphere generated by the huge crowds during performances was similar to that of a large sporting event today. Think football match or the fervour of the Olympic Games. The comparison is apt in many ways for the Elizabethan audience must have been noisier and less well-behaved than today's theatre-goers. They no doubt voiced their approval *and* disapproval more openly. They certainly ate and drank throughout performances, so vendors of food and ale would weave through the crowds, plying their trade, not to mention pick-pockets, pimps and prostitutes doing the same. Apparently, sites of the old Bankside theatres, when excavated, have revealed layer upon layer of crushed nutshells left from the snacking of the early playgoers.

This doesn't mean that they didn't know how to listen – they were probably *much* better at it than we are today. Originally they were called *auditors*, not spectators, and they went to *hear* a play, which shows how much the skill of listening and being transported by the words into other worlds of imagination was a big part of the whole experience. Today we live in such a visual world and are so used to images around us all the time that we are undoubtedly *less* good at concentrating on the spoken word, especially in long speeches. Though we do still have radio drama, of minority interest, where you are completely free to build up a picture of the characters and scene for yourself.

Nowadays, too, most people are so attuned to *individual*, armchair entertainment, online, watching TV, playing electronic games and so on, and are often more familiar with this than they are with big crowd events, such as theatre, sporting matches or concerts for different genres of music. Being part of a large audience still gives a sense of sharing and of group participation, which often heightens the experience emotionally so that you are swept along with all that is happening, being, literally, *taken out of yourself*. It's important to remember that this enhancement of pleasure was a key aspect of theatrical experience for the Elizabethans, just as it is today when you go to see a play or any crowd entertainment, for that matter.

But to return to Will's part in delivering the new entertainment of his time, we'll never know how soon he added writing to his job description, working on his own plays in the evenings. During the hectic daytime rehearsals he may have helped out by making improvements to the script, revising an old play, adding or cutting lines, editing out the tedious bits, tweaking a speech or two. No doubt he had a natural facility for improving a play and making it work better on stage, a talent that the players in his company would soon come to appreciate. Say, for example, you had a good comedian in the company – and there were several brilliant comic actors who became well known, like Robert Armin and Will Kempe – you'd naturally want to give him more material to get extra laughs on stage. Was Will was your man for developing the clowning, adding witty banter, topical jokes or, perhaps, a totally fresh scene of horseplay which would have 'em rolling in the aisles? Very likely. The players would, no doubt, love the improvements he was making to their scripts: *God's bodkins, Will, you ol' rogue, what knavery!* (I've just made up this bit of Elizabethan English.) They probably soon found out that he could do serious, too, writing lines worth saying, lines to manipulate the emotions of the audience...

The old Elizabethan plays, not to mention many of the new ones being written, were in a constant state of flux, being altered to suit the times, the different audiences and venues, or just practicalities like the number of actors available. Some of the old, tatty and dog-eared scripts, having done the rounds with the travelling players, would be in dire need of a make-over. Many were anonymous and, in any case, there were no copyright laws in those days, so you could re-hash them and improvise new sections. Most were handwritten though a few might have been printed, in short runs, in small booklets called quartos, so-called because they were made up of sheets of paper folded into four sections.

Even some of the plays by university writers might need some adaptation to make them stage-worthy. If Will did some re-writing to hone his skills, then his natural talent would certainly gain from all the practical know-how he was acquiring, the hands-on experience that many of the other playwrights lacked. They may have had university educations but most had never worked in a theatre, let alone acted in front of a noisy crowd of critical playgoers, who knew *a hawk from a handsaw*!

So in the early days, Will probably helped to tweak and patch existing plays to meet the demand for scripts, as well as working on his own. Ultimately it was about the audience. The main test of writing for the theatre was, and still is, whether it works on stage and whether you can sell tickets and get bums on seats. Soon, for Mr. Shakescene, it wasn't just a matter of adding and subtracting, altering the shape of an old play, or collaborating with someone else, but of creating something fresh and new of his own. If Will had started out wanting to act, then he'd accidentally stumbled upon the thing at which he was most talented. On the other hand, writing may always have been his ultimate aim.

Alchemy

It is a truth universally acknowledged that Will used old stories as inspiration, borrowing elements of plots and synthesising them into something much greater than the sum of the parts. To inspire means, literally, to breath in, and Will, as an avid reader, must have breathed in so many tales, fragments of stories which fed his creativity and became the plot for a new play. More to the point, he must have made notes or retained what he read – *t'is in my memory locked* – for future use. Using old material inventively, making it new, different and dramatically effective was tantamount to magic, a *transformation devoutly to be wished*. It was like turning base metal into gold, which was what the alchemists, 15th century magicians-cum-scientists, were trying to do, but never succeeded. Will did!

Once a play had been performed and proved popular with audiences, the script really was like gold. *A palpable hit!* A lot of copying by scribes or the literate members of the troupe was involved: separate parts, called *sides*, were written out for each actor to memorise, usually *without* the other parts, so the players often had no idea, at least to start with, what went in between the bits they had to say and what their cue was to begin speaking.

The script had to be closely guarded by the *book-keeper* of the company, who would store the play carefully in a locked chest in a small room to prevent other companies from stealing it. This is the origin of the term *box office*, still in use at theatres today. Rather like pirated DVDs today, scripts could be stolen and copied, so intense was the rivalry between companies to own a successful play. Sometimes there were fierce quarrels between them, and they went to great lengths to outdo each other, even putting spies in the audience at another company's play. If it was a good one, they'd try to rewrite it from notes and memory!

The actors, themselves, were often poached, too, and many did the rounds of different companies, free-lancing. In Will's early years in London, the different troupes of players came and went, shifting frequently as the popularity of the theatre grew and different patrons came forward to support them. Without the financial help of royalty and nobility, the theatre wouldn't have survived and the new enjoyable art form would not have developed as it did.

Will was probably acting with various different companies and touting some of his early plays around for what was very modest payment initially. But at least he was in work and could afford to keep himself and, perhaps send money home, too, via the Stratford carrier, Will Greenaway. If he had dreamed of writing when at Stratford Grammar School, then, finally he was realising his ambition.

In a nutshell: Early Hits

So, Will starts his career and becomes visible in London. From being a lowly apprentice player, he takes the next small step, but giant creative leap for mankind, and begins writing his own plays. By 1592, the year of Greene's acid comments, Will has probably written, and seen performed, a handful of plays. He is becoming recognisable amongst the relatively small circle of players and writers, who would probably all know each other. He isn't *yet* a famous name with audiences, as the playwright is not seen as being terribly important, and therefore often not mentioned on playbills or published scripts. This is soon to change, however, as Will's plays start to become popular and his name *is* published and soon becomes known to playgoers.

A list of known early plays would include *Love's Labours Lost*, *Two Gentlemen of Verona*, *The Taming of the Shrew*, *Richard III*, *Henry VI Parts 1 and 2*, *Titus Andronicus* and *Romeo and Juliet*, comprising three comedies, three history plays and two very different kinds of tragedy, some more well-known than others to modern audiences. Clearly some experimentation is going on here, an important part of the creative learning process before an artist finds his own way. Will was having a go at different types of plays: indeed, he never stopped trying out new ideas and genres for the rest of his career. Most artists and writers go through an early phase when they are influenced by others, but Will seemed to find his own voice very quickly. In fact, he soon started to make his name with comedies and histories, in particular, and, by choosing this route, he offered something very different from the plays by the most popular dramatist at the time.

6. Enter – and exit – Kit Marlowe

Christopher Marlowe, a university man, had already become a famous name, drawing crowds to see his string of tragedies, like *Tamburlaine, The Jew of Malta* and *Dr Faustus*. He and Will were the same age and I imagine would have met, perhaps even spent some time together and become friends. But it's as if Will deliberately chose to try his writing hand at something different – and even when he later turned to tragedies, they were something else altogether. Marlowe was killed in 1592, at the age of 28, in a pub brawl, arguing over the bill – *a great reckoning in a little room* – or so the story goes. It's more likely he was killed for altogether different reasons.

Who murdered Kit Marlowe? would make a good title for a whodunit. The playwright was almost certainly employed by the justifiably paranoid Elizabeth as a spy to root out Catholic conspiracies on the continent, and he may even have been a double agent. Though there were lots of other writers around, none of them had commanded audiences like Marlowe: Will had possibly lost a friend, but also a rival, as the main competition had been had been removed from the scene.

Compare and contrast

Around the time Marlowe's plays were being performed, Will wrote a couple of tragedies, showing he didn't just do comedy and history. You'd have to go a long way to find two more contrasting plays than *Romeo and Juliet* and *Titus Andronicus*. The romantic tragedy of the star-crossed young lovers from two bitterly feuding families is famous the world over and has been given so many different artistic treatments in, for example, opera, painting, or a musical like *West Side Story*. There are also multiple film versions, among them Zefferelli's (1968) and Baz Lurhmannn's (1996). Of the latter, the director says: *With Romeo and Juliet what I wanted to do was to look at the way in which Shakespeare might make a movie of one of his plays if he was a director. How would he make it? We don't know a lot about Shakespeare, but we do know he would make a 'movie' movie. He was a player. We know about the Elizabethan stage and that he was playing for 3000 drunken punters, from the street sweeper to the Queen of England – and his competition was bear-baiting and prostitution.*

Totally different is the play, *Titus Andronicus*, which is hardly ever performed today because it's so horrific that producers fight shy of it. Attempting to write a gory tragedy like those by the Roman playwright Seneca, or possibly sending up the genre, Will anticipated film directors like Ken Russell and Quentin Tarantino by several hundred years, tapping into the public's bloodthirsty predilections. To produce realistic-looking gore needed at key moments in the play, as, for example, when one of the central characters, Lavinia, has her tongue cut out and her hands removed, the actors would burst pigs' bladders full of animal blood under their clothes.

You'd think that we're pretty attuned to violence in film and electronic games, but *Titus* is the stuff of nightmares. So is Marlowe's take on a morality play, *Dr Faustus,* still performed today, in which the eponymous hero sells his soul to the devil. People have always enjoyed being scared half to death, watching the shocking and gruesome – as long they're not the ones doing the suffering and dying.

Such is art and the illusion that is theatre! But something real came along, something much more scary and horrific, which interrupted Will's rise to fame, at this point. It was to threaten his career and all his hard work, never mind about the enormous gamble he had taken, leaving his family and the life he'd known in Stratford.

INTERLUDE

Early success put on hold!

Just as Will was starting to make a name for himself, writing for one or more of the companies of players in London, life as he knew it came to an end.

The plague struck! It was one of the worst outbreaks for years.

Of all the threats to the new theatres and those who worked in them, there was no arguing with the plague. The Puritans and the City Fathers might condemn the theatre as a bad influence, but its popularity with the highest in the land, the Queen and court, meant that most protests didn't get very far. A plague epidemic was a different matter. Events where huge numbers of people congregated meant certain danger of the disease spreading. So when it struck in 1593, all the theatres were immediately closed down. They remained closed for a year.

Imagine an illness which is so lethal that the victim is usually dead in three days. It starts with some sneezing, a rash, a fever; then the *buboes* appear. These are tennis-ball sized swellings in the neck, armpits and groin. They turn red, angry-looking. If they burst or are lanced, mucus and black blood spurt out. The pain is intense and the sufferer quickly becomes delirious, vomiting blood, then longing to sleep. Nine times out of ten, this sleep is their last.

Nowadays pandemics still break out in different parts of the world and defy modern medicine, but the most appalling are usually reserved for the worlds of science fiction and horror movies. We're lucky by comparison with the Elizabethans who lived their lives in the shadow of this infection, *Sir Pest,* as it was sometimes called.

The Black Death, or bubonic plague, spread across Europe in the Middle Ages, mowing down swathes of people. During Will's lifetime it was still a huge killer, especially in the towns and the crowded city of London. For actors, of course, their livelihood was taken away every time the theatres closed and, unless they went travelling, they had no opportunity to practise their art for months at a time. Will's career was affected at various times by serious plague outbreaks.

Apart from knowing that the plague spread rapidly, especially in densely populated areas, people were pretty ignorant about the disease. They thought it was air-born. They didn't know that the blood-sucking fleas, living on black rats, carried the deadly virus and passed it on to any humans they bit. With no proper drainage or sewerage systems, there were a lot of rats and, therefore, a lot of fleas. The plague was highly contagious, passed between humans through the breath or coughing.

They *did* know that poor hygiene was *somehow* connected, and tried to keep their houses clean and scented with sweet-smelling herbs, but the infection was relentless, especially in hot weather. The richer people, including the court, would move out to the countryside, trying to outrun the plague, but most ordinary people had to stay where their home and their work was.

In the outbreak of 1573, over 12,000 Londoners died.

At the end of *Romeo and Juliet*, when the Duke says to the warring families: *A plague on both your houses!* he is not speaking lightly, nor using an empty threat.

Often whole families would suffer and die in rapid succession; crosses were painted on the doors of the victims' houses to warn others to keep away and their bodies were collected at night and tipped into mass graves or plague pits. Victims may have been visited by a plague doctor who could do very little to help, in most cases, except to isolate them. A scary figure, he was clad in a kind of anti-contamination suit – long robes and a helmet with a long bird's beak stuffed with herbs, to avoid breathing the foul air – quite effective protection. Isolating the victims helped, but otherwise people just had to wait for the terrible disease to run its course. Eventually an epidemic would die out of its own accord, sometimes when the weather turned colder.

Most people today are lucky enough not to know what trying to survive with a clear and present danger is like, unless they have lived in a time of war. The constant threat of suffering and death must mean that you are on high alert all the time, in a state of constant fear. Sometimes people develop an attitude of recklessness, a desire to live life to the full, for *tomorrow ye die*. The following poem, written in 1592, as part of a play, called *Summer's Last Will and Testament*, gives a sense of the horror of living in a time of plague.

A Litany in Time of Plague
Thomas Nashe

Adieu, farewell, earth's bliss;
This world uncertain is;
Fond are life's lustful joys;
Death proves them all but toys;
None from his darts can fly;
I am sick, I must die.
Lord, have mercy on us!

Rich men, trust not in wealth,
Gold cannot buy you health;
Physic himself must fade.
All things to end are made,
The plague full swift goes by;
I am sick, I must die.
Lord, have mercy on us!

Beauty is but a flower
Which wrinkles will devour;
Brightness falls from the air;
Queens have died young and fair;
Dust hath closed Helen's eye.
I am sick, I must die.
Lord, have mercy on us!

Strength stoops unto the grave,
Worms feed on Hector brave;
Swords may not fight with fate,
Earth still holds open her gate.
"Come, come!" the bells do cry.

I am sick, I must die.
Lord, have mercy on us!

Wit with his wantonness
Tasteth death's bitterness;
Hell's executioner
Hath no ears for to hear
What vain art can reply.
I am sick, I must die.
Lord, have mercy on us!

Haste, therefore, each degree,
To welcome destiny;
Heaven is our heritage,
Earth but a player's stage;
Mount we unto the sky.
I am sick, I must die.
Lord, have mercy on us!

Will was probably in London during some of this horrendous plague year – and again was spared, just as he had avoided the Stratford outbreak as a baby. Perhaps he stayed in his room writing – but he'd still have to venture out for food; maybe he left the city with his fellow actors. It's also possible he spent some of the year at home with his wife and family, or at one of the houses of his new, aristocratic patron.

In those days there were no government hand-outs, sick payments or unemployment benefits; the Welfare State was four hundred years in the future. Out-of-work actors had to take to the road to earn a precarious living, performing in towns and villages, as they had done before the coming of the theatres. The alternative was starvation – for them and their dependants.

If Will returned home for part of the plague year, perhaps it was an unlooked for happy time, especially if he'd been able to save some money; evidence suggests that Will was careful financially. But I keep coming back in my imagination to the polarity of Will's life. After the crazy, hectic time in London, did it feel weird to be back home again? Did he find it difficult to reassume his roles of son, husband, father – the other half of his double life – as if nothing had happened? I can imagine him regaling everyone with stories of his new life, enacting speeches for them, showing them scripts... Will sometimes referred to actors as *shadows* – insubstantial, changing shape, protean. Did he begin to wonder if his short-lived success had all been a dream?

Will turns serious poet

If he did, he managed to move on, career-wise. He was nothing if not resourceful and adaptable to circumstances. Will did what he did best – continued writing: not plays this time, because there was little incentive, with the theatres all closed, but two long, narrative love poems. The irony is that the poems, *Venus and Adonis* and *The Rape of Lucrece,* which are hardly read at all now, probably brought him more money than playwriting did. They definitely helped him to make friends in high places and influence people.

To understand how he did this, you need to know a bit more about the system of Elizabethan patronage, a kind of early form of social media – and how it worked. Rather like business and sponsorship today, rich noblemen wanted recognition and self-promotion, so they would pay writers for dedicating their work to them, thus ensuring some fame for themselves for posterity. Writers offered a kind of eternity, just as much as portraits, marble tombs and monuments preserved the memory of those who were well-born or famous in their own lifetimes.

Will's target audience this time was very different from the broad sweep of social classes at which his plays were aimed. His poems were for educated readers, young men, and some women, too, who couldn't get enough love poetry and enjoyed all verse fashions, like the sonnet, coming out of Italy. Containing some salacious sexual detail, Will's poems especially appealed to the university students who acclaimed *sweet Mr Shakespeare* as the best thing since the discovery of tobacco!

Will dedicated his poems to the young Earl of Southampton, Henry Wriothsley, (pronounced *Rizzley*), whom he had probably met or seen at the theatre. In the conventional self-abasement mode which sounds a bit smarmy to us today, he penned a dedication of fulsome praise: *The love I dedicate to your lordship is without end..... What I have done is yours; what I have to do is yours...*

It certainly did the trick. Those were days of rigid class division when grovelling was the name of the game. Researchers think that the young Earl and Will became friends and that Will visited Southampton's house at Tichfield, becoming the equivalent of an in-house writer, and was paid well for his allegiance. He may even have travelled abroad with the Earl, perhaps to Italy, which became the setting for many of his later plays. There's no evidence for this, apart from the plays themselves, only speculation.

You could say that Will was an opportunist and that the plague helped to boost his career, as the publication of the two poems proved he was a serious writer, not just a *playmaker*. It seems strange today that not only did poems earn more money, but they were also held in much higher regard than plays, even ones written in iambic verse, as was the fashion, but this was the case. Once again, Will seemed to have acted with a sure instinct for success and once again he had usurped the position of the university-educated poets! And proved he had his finger on the popular pulse, albeit that belonging to a different segment of society.

His plays had no doubt already attracted the attention of noble and wealthy theatre-goers, but, with the endorsement of his poems by Southampton, his star was definitely rising in the upper class firmament. What isn't always realised is that this year could have been a turning point in his career: he might have continued to write more poetry for the young Earl or perhaps have been offered a position in his household, as a secretary, possibly – we don't know whether the option was there. But there is some evidence of a quarrel between Will and Southampton, which was later made up. Whatever the truth, having a patron was certainly one of the ways a young man of humble birth might find a secure job, as well as the means to ascend the social ladder. It could even have led to an intro to Elizabeth's court and a position as a royal servant. Will might have never returned to the theatre.

Just imagine, if Will had stayed in the household of the Earl, he'd probably just be known today as one of many minor Elizabethan poets, writing under noble patronage, and as the author of a handful of successful plays!

Was this a bigger crossroads in his life than biographers think? Whatever happened, or didn't happen, Will had got lucky again. By good judgment and initiative, he'd managed to benefit from an outbreak of plague and the closing of all the theatres.

ACT FOUR:

The Naughty Nineties

1. 1594 Theatres reopen after huge death toll!

The last decade of the 16th century was for many a roistering, rollicking, rumbustious one, in all sorts of ways, as life got back to normal after the plague and the theatres rocked. It was definitely a roller-coaster ride for Will: he was climbing up to the heights of his fame and achievement, but something also happened in the 1590s which brought him crashing down and changed his life for ever.

The decade started with the defeat of the Spanish Armada: patriotism reached a high as the fear of invasion receded. The nineties ended with yet another unsuccessful rebellion against the Queen.

The theatres had reopened and were drawing huge audiences again, even though some acting troupes must have been depleted by the plague epidemic. As for plays, old favourites were performed along with the more recent successes of Will Shakespeare and his contemporary, Kit Marlowe, but new ones were always needed. The law of supply and demand came into operation; the more people wanted to see plays, the busier the writers became. There were to be many new dramatists on the block in the coming years and competition between them, like the rivalry between players, was fierce. Will was probably more than happy to return to the theatre after the plague outbreak; whether his relationship with Southampton remained strong or not, perhaps writing fulsome dedications to young noblemen was not where his heart lay and he wanted to get his teeth into some stronger meat, acting again and writing plays. Perhaps narrative poetry didn't quicken his pulses in the way that live theatre did. Financially, the time-out had done him no harm – one of the early biographers speaks of a large gift of money from Southampton, in addition to the earnings from his poetry.

So Will was back in show business, his career inextricably linked with the continuing rise of the drama which was to flourish well into the 17th century, halted eventually by the English Civil War, the execution of an anointed king, and the ensuing period of Puritan power when all the theatres were all closed down.

New acting company formed!

Will returned to the life he'd led before the plague years had temporarily halted his stage career. The fact that a new acting company, *The Lord Chamberlain's Men,* was formed in 1594, at just the right time, may have had something to do with his reasoning. Will got lucky again. After several years in London, working for different companies, he and some of the best actors joined forces, under the patronage of the Lord Chamberlain, Lord Hunsden, an important court official, who would give them prestige and entry into high circles. Probably Will had already worked with many of the company, in particular the Burbages: Richard Burbage, the son of James Burbage, another theatre manager like Henslow, was one of the most talented actors of his times, only equalled by his rival in another company, Edward Alleyn. Both became celebrities of the day and drew huge crowds when they were taking the lead roles in plays. Will and Richard met up at just the right time and the former was to write many amazing parts for Burbage, who must have excelled at playing characters like Hamlet, King Lear, Richard II, Shylock, Prospero and many more. It's interesting to note that Will's protagonists became gradually older later in his writing career, as he and Richard Burbage themselves aged.

The Lord Chamberlain's Men became Will's colleagues, close companions and friends. They were to stay together for the rest of Will's working life, performing his plays and giving him the stability he needed to develop his talent. Will was a vital member of the group, both as their chief writer and also, according to original cast lists, as an actor, too. This was a time when many of the formerly shifting troupes of players became more stable and established; with more purpose-built theatres, acting companies had less need to travel around the country from one venue to another, though most of them, including *The Lord Chamberlain's Men*, did still take to the roads at times and give performances in other towns.

In spite of the popularity of play-going, overall control rested with the court, which meant the Queen. Fortunately Elizabeth loved the theatre, too, so she played a key role in helping it to flourish and over-ruled all the objections which came from two quarters – the City Fathers and the Puritans. The former, a kind of City Council, took the line that the theatres caused civil mayhem, and increased crime, never mind about the danger of plague breaking out where such huge groups of people were gathered together. The latter, strictly religious, believed in stamping out all the *impurities* of the old Catholic religion, hence their name. They also believed fervently that plays were sinful and corrupt.

Elizabeth never went to the theatre – the theatre always came to her! The leading companies could be summoned at any time of year to play before Her Majesty in one of her many palaces. During holiday times like Christmas, for example, she would command a number of different performances for the court's entertainment and her own *solace and pleasure*, as she expressed it. *The Lord Chamberlain's Men* became one of her favourite companies and Will's plays, which they mostly performed, became very popular in court circles as well as in the theatres. What a coup for the new company and Will! Not only would they would be paid well for their services, but they were to become regular visitors to the royal palaces and accustomed to meeting many of the influential nobles and courtiers who attended their performances.

No one knows how soon Will became personally known to the Queen as the resident writer of *The Lord Chamberlain's Men*, or if indeed he did, though it seems likely. Perhaps he was a favourite with Elizabeth – after all, he was a good-looking young man of thirty who was well able to get on with the rich and powerful, as he had proved by gaining Southampton as a patron. I would imagine that he could talk the talk, engaging in witty repartee till the cows came home for milking across England's green and pleasant land. However, he never became *Sir William*: funny how knighthoods seemed to go to all the roistering soldiers and sailors, like Sir Walter Raleigh and Sir Francis Drake! With his wonderfully macho name, *Shakespeare*, you'd have thought the Queen would have made an exception for Will, but I don't think play-writing and acting were yet considered important enough to qualify for such honours. However, the royal favour shown to the company did their reputation no harm at all – in the capital, the country, and beyond. It's known that travellers from Europe would come to see plays in the London theatres, having heard of their fame, and indeed, one of few surviving sketches of a theatre building, *The Swan*, is by a Dutchman, Johannes de Witt.

Not all plays on the public stage were seen by the Queen, but a play couldn't be performed until passed by the court official called the Master of Revels. What a splendid job title to put on your CV – *Master of Revels*! To be serious, however, his job included strict censorship, looking for anything subversive which might mean danger to her Majesty. Political correctness is not a new concept – it just had more serious implications in Elizabethan England where it could literally be a matter of life and death for the offender. The written word in plays, poetry and pamphlets represented the only kind of media in those days – there were no newspapers even – and it had to be scrutinised very carefully, especially in plays, because they reached such a wide audience. One of Ben Jonson's works, called *The Isle of Dogs* (snappy title), was banned and never performed. I'd love to know what was too shocking or dangerous for the Elizabethan audience to see it, but no copies have survived.

A day in the life...

Out of all the men (and it was all men at this stage) involved in making the new art form so popular, Will had *more* connections with *more* elements of it than anyone else. First of all he was both a writer *and* an actor. This dual role was unusual – few actors wrote plays as well, or vice versa – and gave him a unique position of control within the company. Experts think that he would have been closely involved with the *direction* of productions, too, during the morning rehearsals, as there was no official director in those days. For a company to have their chief writer in their midst must have given them a considerable advantage: the actors could be advised and guided by him, having his intentions clarified, regarding the play in rehearsal, as it took shape. All members of the company would be interdependent, relying heavily on each other, working as a team for every performance. In addition there were the young apprentices to look after and train up. One big family, then, but like all families, things would flow smoothly at times, and less smoothly at others. There must have been camaraderie, friendship and deep loyalty, but also the inevitable quarrels, jealousies and rivalries.

The players usually put on a different play each day – no pressure there, then. For Will, there would be his own part to learn and the other actors to direct, as well as inevitable alterations and rewrites to do as rehearsals went along. Then there was the major part of his work – the writing of brand *new* plays for the repertoire – which would involve working long into the night, when everyone else was in their beds. The pace must have been relentless: writing, rehearsing and performing, for the entertainment of commoner and courtier alike, to provide a livelihood for himself and all the members of the *Lord Chamberlain's Men*. No doubt there were lots of days for Will, when 24 hours were not enough. His was a high-octane job.

On top of this, Will was a *sharer* in the new company, in effect a stakeholder: several key members including Will and Richard Burbage, made a legal agreement to run the company together and share the profits between them, after expenses and wages had been paid. This initiative subsequently became a new model for theatre management and one which would incentivise everyone to make a good income. Obviously it was dependent on box office takings ... more pressure! Like any business, it needed to be managed efficiently with careful book-keeping. Writing successful plays *alone* did not bring in serious cash: plays were not considered a very high form of literature, even popular ones, so playwrights got a raw deal, considering they were so crucial to the process. But running a successful acting company – that *was* fast becoming a money-spinner. The new, democratic business model for this band of players sounds modern, even to us today: in Will's time it represented a huge step forward for acting troupes, making them much more professional and, earning them more money and status.

If you feel exhausted just thinking about Will's daily workload, then I wouldn't blame you. Was it his dream job? Aye, by God's holy trousers! Did he thrive on it? Methinks he did! Clearly he had loads of energy and wasn't afraid of hard work, though, like most jobs, there would have been moments of tedium and frustration, when even Will had a bad day at the office. With public performance being the *be-all and end-all*, there must have been constant crises to avert or overcome, and even days when complete melt-down seemed very close. We talk about jobs with long hours and high stress levels today; Will kept up a relentless pace, for the next few years, completing an average of two to three plays a year for *The Lord Chamberlain's Men.* How on earth did he manage to write so many plays of such high quality in the time available, especially when it was show-time most days of the week?

2. *In my mind's eye:* A Pound of Flesh 1597

Even the Thames has frozen over. London lies under a coverlet of snow which renders everything peaceful and pure. Will is stabbed to the soul with the beauty of it all.

Back in his lodgings, he warms weary limbs by the fire, sipping from a stoop of spiced ale, brought up by the scrawny pot boy who looks half-starved with cold, poor fellow. Belike he's eleven or twelve years old, roughly the same age as his own son ...

Will tries to choke down his sadness, to swallow grief, which at times seems to affect his whole being and identity. He must drag his thoughts back to the business in hand. He still has some key speeches to fashion anew, and some comic lines to re-jig before the fire burns low.

His Jewish play is going well. He feels it in his bones. Richard Burbage, that consummate actor, is growing into the character of Shylock with his usual amazing empathy – he and Will inspire each other now. Strange how they both seem to feel for this underdog, for this bitter moneylender from the despised race. Why is there always such hatred for Jews? Will thinks of the dreadful case of the Portuguese Jew, Ruy Lopez, almost certainly innocent of treason yet given the worst of deaths at Tyburn.

'If you prick us, do we not bleed? If you tickle us, do we not laugh? If you poison us, do we not die?'

Will tingles with the unique excitement that comes when words he has crafted will, he knows, reach deep into the hearts of his audience. The Jew is disgraced, of course, and beautiful Portia triumphs, finding the man of her dreams, that's romantic comedy for you, but... There's always a 'but' in Will's mind. Nothing is ever clear-cut like the preaching of the Puritans or the pompous prattle of those who never entertain self-doubt. Will has always found it easy to become deeply involved with his characters: he can get inside Shylock's head: he understands the verities of the Jew's life – money mainly, but racial pride, too, and, above all, hatred, like a canker grown. After years of ill treatment, bitterness has festered and become something monstrous... so why not ask for a pound of flesh, for God's sake? Why not insist on such a shocking bond? T'is apt for revenge...

But for all that, Shylock is still human. He has some soul. Let the playgoers, themselves, sit in judgment at the court scene he's written.

This so-called comedy has become something different again, for Will: a comedy to be taken seriously. Not akin to anything else he's written so far. But he trusts his instinct. There's more to comedy than fun and fooling, love and happy outcomes, all of which please the play-goers, of course. Let light contend with darkness. Contrast is all, as the humblest painter's apprentice knows. He moves to his table and picks up his pen.

He is writing for all underdogs and all outsiders, when he crafts the character of the Jew, gives Shylock flesh. (No pun intended, but a good play on words, nonetheless!) Of course, he is writing for his audience too — to entertain them, naturally, but to offer them something more to reflect on, to talk about with their friends. Something different from the usual entrenched antipathies. He is writing for Richard who will take his lines to the playgoers and bring that roar of applause that tells him his play lives and thrives.

Fate has brought him this company of good actors with their powerful patron, the Lord Chamberlain. All they need now is their own theatre. During the Yuletide season just past, they played seven times at court. Seven different plays before the Queen. Elizabeth shimmered like a goddess with her jewels and lace, the dress of finest silk spread wide, almost holding her up. Her armour. S'blood, t'is said she owns over thirty thousand dresses! She may have the body of a weak and feeble woman, but she knows how to disguise it. As she told her soldiers before the Armada of Spanish ships fell into disarray, she has the 'heart and stomach of a man'. She knows how to pen a speech too. Will respects that above all. It's his life's blood and his livelihood! Ha! The Queen loves to play on words, too!

But she is becoming old. The ghastly white face is painted an inch thick. Perched on top, the red wig and crown look grotesque, seen close to.

Gloriana! Good Queen Bess! 'The imperial votress', Will called her in A Midsummer Night's Dream, in delicate reference to her supposed chastity, the act that has become part of her lifelong performance. Confound her, she can't still be a virgin after all that dalliance with Leicester and my lord, Essex!

Will writes on swiftly. The sheer joy of words, words, words... he doesn't count them. He's always been able to write quickly, fluently: the blank verse rarely halts. As long as there are about two hours traffic upon the stage... Forsooth, he has an instinct he can rely on, but that doesn't stop him re-writing when something's out of joint, changing the merest detail if he needs to. The rigour of his schooldays has never left him.

His thoughts have now left the English court hundreds of miles away and in his mind's eye he is looking down on a wide canal in Venice, as shown by the famous Italian painters. The grand bridge is bedecked with banners and flags, lined with topsy-turvy shops, crowded with people like a marketplace. He imagines the babble of voices, the warmth of the sun, the vivid colours. The Rialto. 'What news on the Rialto?'

3. Variety is the spice of life

It's usually agreed that Will's dramatic output falls loosely into 3 phases:

- Comedies and Histories

- Tragedies

- The Late Romances – plays which don't fall precisely into any of the above three categories

It's a good, general starting point, but not that simple. Will's plays can't all be neatly pigeonholed into phases for different genres: he mixed it up, experimented, not always successfully, and paid some heed to the vagaries and fashions of the times, but was not in thrall to them. Life's *infinite variety* was what interested him and what he wanted to turn into art. He never got in a rut, he never stopped still and he never got left behind. There are some problem plays which no-one knows how to categorize and the fact that there are exceptions to every generalisation about Will's plays shows how varied his writing was. He tried something, than went in for something completely different. He wasn't an artist who painted the same picture every time. He also developed, changed, matured – as most creative artists do. His wit never deserted him, but his insight grew as he worked.

It's risky, however, to try and link episodes of Will's life with his work – though most biographers do get drawn into this, and I'm as guilty as the next one. Experts also try and infer stuff about Will as a person from his plays – you only have to read them to know that his soul is in his words – but therein lurks danger. You always have to remind yourself that Will was writing to entertain audiences for a living. The age of personal writing, of wearing your heart on your sleeve, came later with Wordsworth and his famous daffodils.

I can sense you nodding off: *I will be brief,* as Polonius, one of Will's tedious old fool characters, says, even though he's quite incapable of cutting a long story short.

There is general agreement about the rough order in which the plays were written, but no one knows for sure, and there is always hot debate amongst academics, who enjoy this kind of wrangling. All would agree that Will's tragic period, for which he is generally most famous, came later in his career, except for *Romeo and Juliet,* which he'd already written... oh, and *Titus Andronicus.....* See what I mean about the difficulty of putting his plays into boxes.

But, apart from these, the first two genres listed, history and comedy, were the ones with which Will initially made his name in the London theatre.

4. A Sense of History and a Sense of Humour

Experts know, from Philip Henslowe's records, that Will's history plays drew large audiences at *The Rose* as people were drawn to stories of their monarchy and past wars, as many of us still are. Today, it seems to me, history has never been more popular, evidenced by books, documentaries and whole TV channels devoted to the subject, not to mention the many films, novels and TV dramas which are set in different historical periods. At the time of writing, the recent news story of the discovery of Richard III's body below a car park in Leicester has excited the English nation. This monarch, the last Plantagenet king, who died a violent death in battle, was the subject of one of Will's first plays about English history and it enthralled the Elizabethan playgoers. He was to write many more about the Wars of the Roses and the Tudor dynasty, drawing on Ralph Holinshed's Chronicles for source material, but giving his own take on what had happened and fleshing out the central characters. He also wrote Roman history plays, the most famous being *Julius Caesar* and *Antony and Cleopatra.*

Alongside the histories, many of Will's first plays were romantic comedies with happily-ever-after endings. In the frenetically busy period in the 1590s, up to the Queen's death in 1603, Will wrote a whole string of comedies, many of which are well known and often performed today: *The Taming of the Shrew, A Midsummer Night's Dream, A Comedy of Errors, Much Ado about Nothing, As you Like it, The Merchant of Venice and Twelfth Night.* With his *ready wit,* he was a natural at comedy, though these plays aren't just about humour.

They usually involve characters from a long-ago world – princes, dukes, princesses, magicians, fairies, jesters and so forth – but they are up to date and familiar to us in terms of the main theme (romantic love) and the mood (light-hearted, funny, up-beat). The essential plot is familiar, too: boy meets girl, all sorts of problems beset them, but eventually the lovers are united. The audience sympathise, but at the same time can laugh (because it's a comedy) at the mess that the characters get themselves into. Compare the standard themes and story-lines of modern *rom-coms,* like *Notting Hill,* that are such big box-office hits, and you'll find that they're pretty similar to Will's comedies. Will included high comedy (witty dialogue) and low comedy (slapstick), along with various plot-twists, misunderstandings and improbable coincidences – again, not so very different from modern romantic comedies. Nor were the characters, the young people at the centre of the drama, very far removed from today's heroes and heroines. *The course of true love never did run smooth:* Will used this premise again and again as the basis for all sorts of fun and games in his comedies.

He could also change the mood. He was adept at creating a smooth transition between the comic and serious at the drop of a bejewelled velvet hat. Take his main theme – love. He can mock the fluffy hearts and flowers bit to create humour and show how ridiculous love and doting lovers can be, but, when he's being serious about the subject, you know instantly. He can ramp up the language, so that you totally empathise with the very real feelings of the main characters – which suddenly become more important than all the crazy twists and turns of the plot. Educated or not, those watching and listening would recognise the heart-stopping moment, like Rosalind's declaration in *As You Like It:*

O coz, coz, coz, my pretty little coz, that thou didst know how many fathom deep I am in love!

To say that Will understands what love feels like would be an understatement: he's been there, done it, and bought several *hempen homespun* t-shirts.

As he became more confident in this genre, Will began to write comedies of more depth, with more rounded characters, breaking down the boundaries between the comic and tragic genres. He knew that the other side of the clown's face is sad, weeping real tears, and that comedy can potentially turn to tragedy. Ultimately, Will's mature comedies aren't just about humorous mistakes and romance leading to happy-ever-after marriages: they go deeper, making you think, too, just as good comedy does today.

Closet feminist?

But where did Will get his amazing feisty female characters from? These intelligent, resourceful young women who feel so modern, who can articulate their feelings so wonderfully? Who take on the men, in the battles between the sexes, and usually win hands down, especially where emotional intelligence, as it's called today, is concerned. No other writers at the time created female characters like these wise, brave, beautiful but not too perfect women, who are capable of *growing* and being changed by the events of the play. In many contemporary plays, (and some of Will's early ones), the heroines were more stereotypical, token characters, important for the plot but not for themselves; in his best comedies, Will's women are spikey and fun but also feminine. Did he know women like Rosalind, Beatrice and Portia, from his double life of home and away, or did his male fantasy create them out of thin air? Later, in his tragedies, he was to create even more memorable women, like Lady Macbeth and Cleopatra. The men in the audience must have loved them, but so must the female theatre-goers, who could identify with so much that they said and did. A win-win situation, then, four hundred years before feminism.

For all that, it was still a man's world, in spite of the strong, fiercely intelligent female monarch and the many nobly born, well educated women at court who could hold their own intellectually. Well born women rarely held positions of power and had only their marriageability as an asset, which in turn was dependent on wealth and looks. Lower down the social scale similar patterns applied: women were little more than chattels according to the marriage laws and, though there were undoubtedly some love matches, many alliances were much more pragmatic, based on convenient arrangements between families of similar social standing or trades. Will knew this of course, but, showed his characters achieving the dream of romantic love most of us aspire to. He *was* in the entertainment business, after all, and escapism is vital in any age, but especially when life was often, to quote another Elizabethan, Thomas Hobbes, *nasty, brutish and short.*

Another irony was that women were not yet allowed to act on the public stages. So these amazing heroines were played by young pre-pubescent boys – a fact which takes a bit of getting your head around! They were well trained and often very skilful, bewigged and wearing skirts, at playing female characters. Men in drag, they were not. When you get to know some of Will's comedies you find that he includes lots of opportunities in the story-line for his leading ladies to be disguised as young men – Portia, Viola, Rosalind, all pretend to be men for a considerable part of the play. What the Elizabethan audience saw, then, was a young man (the actor), playing a woman, who for much of the play is disguised as a man. Layers of irony are built up, which must have added to the fun, not to mention given an added sexual frisson, for both sexes in the audience. The cross-dressing and gender-bending are still very funny on stage today, but lack the extra nuance of the first performances, inevitably. A few modern producers have tried all-male versions of Will's plays with some success, and this is the closest we can get to understanding what it must have been like in that long-ago world of Elizabethan theatre.

A Midsummer Night's Dream

How funny are the comedies?

Wit, an't be thy will, put me into good fooling! says Feste, the professional clown in *Twelfth Night,* hoping to keep his job with the Countess, Olivia.

I think if Will had been writing comic scripts today, maybe for film or TV, as well as for the stage, he'd have been hugely successful, with his quick ear, observational skills and rapier wit. Not to mention the understanding of human nature which feeds into all his art and makes us laugh at the ridiculousness of human behaviour. Because the tragedies are so famous, Will's talent for comedy is sometimes overlooked, but his characters and their plights have a timelessness about them. The comedies still have the potential to be made very funny in productions today the world over. The things you laugh at stay the same for the most part, whatever age you live in. It's the verbals which cause a few problems because in 450 years language has changed and in-jokes, colloquialisms and topical gags disappear over months and years, never mind about decades and centuries. Comedy doesn't always stand the test of time – think of some TV sitcoms which seem very unfunny years later.

The Elizabethans loved the cut and thrust of word play, the verbal equivalent of the fencing matches they so enjoyed. It contained lots of the stuff that makes us laugh today – fast repartee, gags, innuendo, double-entendre, one-liners, put-downs, understatement and exaggeration. Puns were very popular – and there are thousands in Will's plays, sometimes loaded with sexual meaning, which has always been a good way for comic writers and comedians to include smut and obscenity in a subtle way. But, if you're reading one of Will's plays and you have to refer to footnotes every other word, it can become very tedious. A joke that has to be explained usually ceases to be funny. I remember when studying *Hamlet* at school, a rather coy footnote explained that the line *'Did you think I meant **country** matters?'* contained *a pun on the obscene word for the female pudendum.* What? I probably knew the c-word but I certainly didn't know the word *pudendum,* so was none the wiser regarding this 16th century fanny joke!

It's true, however, that a good modern-day production of a Shakespearean comedy with skilled actors can still bring out the verbal comedy in a way which doesn't seem possible when you are reading it on the page, where it can become dull and tedious.

Bring on the Clowns!

For one thing, there are so many different types of humour to be found In Shakespeare's comedies – not just the verbal sort. Think popular sit-coms on TV today with their range from less sophisticated situation comedy – farce, pratfalls, slapstick – to the more cerebral modes of irony and satire. Will does these, too, for his huge audience from all levels of society. He also creates a wide variety of memorable comic characters during the course of his career, from rustics and revellers, fops and pedants, buffoons and clowns, to the professional or *licensed* fools, based on the traditional court jester figure, like Richard Tarlton, the Queen's jester.

One of Will's best known comic characters is Bottom in *A Midsummer Night's Dream*, who literally has an ass's head put on him as a joke – everyone else sees it but he doesn't. In a different vein is the creation of Falstaff who provides comic relief (virtually invented by Shakespeare) in two of the history plays, and was said to have been one of the Queen's all-time favourite characters. In Will's later plays, his licensed fool characters, always more witty and intelligent than the hapless Bottom, developed and changed, becoming more wise, sometimes sad, too. Experts have discovered that the comedian and dancer, Will Kempe, one of the original sharers, left The Lord Chamberlain's Men around 1600, possibly after a disagreement, and that Robert Armin, a different, more subtle kind of comic actor, joined the troupe of players, probably inspiring Will to create parts, like Touchstone in *As You Like It*, Feste in *Twelfth Night* and the Fool in *King Lear*, to suit his more alternative style.

In most acting troupes, there were specialist comic actors, who could lift the lines off the page – no comic script works without a good comedian to bring it alive which Will knew only too well and he could, no doubt, picture Kempe or Armin playing a part as he created it.

Dumbing down?

Will seems to have had the knack of writing comedy which was universally popular: it's easy to imagine that the coarser comedy was directed more at the *groundlings* and that the verbal comedy was for the more educated in the audience. Undoubtedly, there was some truth in this, but this is to assume the groundlings were thick – which they weren't. They probably missed some of the more precious verbal jokes or some of the literary references, but they were just as capable of being moved to tears of laughter or sadness as the young students or courtiers. So, no, I don't think Will thought in terms of dumbing down, rather of mixing it up and including different types of comedy, something for everyone.

He also included comedy in his tragedies, breaking the tension temporarily, and diverging from the concept of tragedy as conceived by the classical writers. It's often just as funny – sometimes more so – than the humour in the comedies, though later generations of playgoers didn't always agree and in the 18th century scenes like the porter's scene in *Macbeth* were cut. No modern producer would think of cutting the graveyard scene in *Hamlet*, and depriving the audience of the two gravediggers, joking inappropriately about their trade, and unearthing bones and skulls all over the stage, as they prepare Ophelia's grave. Black comedy or gallows humour is nothing new.

The Magic of Music

As with comedy, the songs Will includes in many of his comedies work much better on stage, adding to the atmosphere and mood. If you're reading a play, you'll frequently come across stage directions and/or one of the characters calling for musicians or instruments, or even for a dance to be performed. For example, *Twelfth Night* starts with the famous injunction of Duke Orsino to his musicians: *If music be the food of love, play on!* In the same play, the clown, Feste, performs several songs for the entertainment of the other characters and the audience, adding another dimension to the mood of this plaintive, bitter-sweet comedy, one of the last that Will wrote of this genre, before he turned to writing tragedy.

If you're studying a play on the page, you tend to skip over the songs – like most song lyrics they can sound a bit naff and they don't seem to add much to the play without the music. Nowadays we tend to regard songs in drama as the preserve of musicals and opera, though we accept the musical score to a film without question. The Elizabethans loved hearing live music, having no means of recording it, as we do, and most of the songs occur naturally within the action of the play, as a singer or musician is asked to perform. However, experts also think it possible that in one of the galleries over the stage there were musicians who would have played background music at certain times, perhaps having the same effect as a film score does. There are also songs in the tragedies: usually linked closely to plot and character, they also have the dramatic effect of heightening the mood, as, for example, Desdemona's *Song of Willow* in *Othello*, which builds almost unbearable tension before her violent murder.

Watching a stage production, with Will's songs set to music, it's so much easier to value their contribution to the mood and themes of the play as a whole.

Scene and Heard

The same goes for appreciating the music of Will's language and poetry. It seems odd to us today to choose to write the play's dialogue in poetry, not in prose, the way people really speak. However, it was a matter of convention at the time, having come down from both classical theatre and from mediaeval religious drama. What *was* new was the choice of *blank verse,* as it was called, an unrhymed poetry with a naturally powerful and flowing metre, *iambic pentameter*, like the rhythm of the heart, a pulse. Though it was originally an Italian fashion, it suited the stresses and intonation of the English language, too, and was adopted by many Elizabethan poets and dramatists. Present-day actors have discussed the need to get into the rhythms of the five-beat blank verse as a key part of the Shakespeare acting experience and most are extremely successful, which shows how flexible this metre can be 450 years after it was written.

At the end of this book, I've included a more detailed section of FAQs on Shakespearean verse form.

In a nutshell: Will's sources

Where did these happy comedies, along with the tragedies and histories, spring from? Were they fully formed in Will's imagination? The short answer is, no. Will was gifted at creating the all-important story-line for each play, but he didn't invent every element of the plot: he utilised old stories. He read anything and everything he could get his hands on and borrowed different bits of old tales, giving them the unique Will treatment and enhancing them way beyond the originals. I can imagine Will enjoying the challenge of devising a good plot with twists and turns, tension and surprise, in the way that novelists or writers for film and TV do today.

Most writers these days have to do some research for background accuracy, and, with the Internet, it can be pretty easy to find what you want, but Will obviously had to get what he needed from books, which he'd beg, buy or borrow, using the printers and booksellers of London, or the libraries of wealthy friends. We know that Will had extremely good Latin, possibly some Greek, (in spite of Ben Jonson's remarks to the contrary) and had read a large number of classical poems and plays at school. He could probably understand French quite well and may have had a working knowledge of Italian. In any case, there were more and more translations of popular books coming onto the market.

Imagine him dipping in and out of old stories, history books, plays, narrative poems, translations, folk tales... He probably jotted down anything that grabbed his attention, details and dates, people and places that piqued his interest, or just remembered them in his actor's well-trained memory. There was certainly method in it. Something he'd read about would eventually become the starting point for a new play, and the whole creative process would begin: imagining, writing and dramatizing. It's difficult to do justice to the part played by Will's imagination and his ability to take elements of old stories, mix them up and transform them so completely, working out a new plot and creating characters all his own.

Many of these stories came from Italy, which partly explains why Will often set his plays there – that and the Elizabethan love affair with everything Italian. When you first look at a list of characters, it can put you off, because of the unfamiliarity of the names, many being Italian, though Will usually added some English ones for good measure. He must have enjoyed inventing comic names, for example those of the duo in *Twelfth Night*, Sir Toby Belch, the glutton and drunkard, and his side-kick, Sir Andrew Aguecheek, a dim-witted knight, rather like Lord Percy in *Blackadder II.*

The main difference in Will's day – apart from the Internet – was that there were no plagiarism laws and it was OK to use an old story as the basis for a new play. Printing was a recent development and more and more books were being published, but nothing like the trillions in print today. Playwrights recycled old plays and stories for the Elizabethan stage and, if they were talented, they created something fresh and new, something imbued with their own vision. Will was undoubtedly the best at spotting a story's potential and blending several different stories into one: he had an unerring instinct for finding material to inspire a new five-act drama, be it comedy, tragedy or history.

Scholars have worked on sources of Will's plays but exactly *what* Will read and *how* it was transformed by his imagination can never be totally known. If you're studying a play text, there's always a note about sources, which can seem dry and academic (in both senses) until you realise what Will was doing. He would mix elements from different bits of reading and make them into something else entirely; like stitching together fabrics from a ragbag of literature to make a brand new quilt, glowing in colour and intricate in design. Even this metaphor doesn't really do justice to Will's unique gift; other Elizabethan playwrights could stitch and sew and refashion too, but none could pull off this magic trick so skilfully, time and time again, play after play.

5. Public and private faces

Way back at the start of this book I suggested that, even to friends and family, Will Shakespeare was possibly something of an enigma. Towards the end of the 1590s when Will was becoming more and more successful, what did everyone think of this talented actor-turned-writer, *the upstart crow* who'd been in London for eight to ten years now?

The public would see a successful playwright, whose name, if not a household one, would be well known amongst keen playgoers of all ranks, as both writer and actor. Adjectives like *sweet* and *honey-tongued* are often used about Will by contemporaries, in appreciation of his mellifluous way with words, especially on the subject of love, the central theme of his comedies. People, no doubt, imagined a happy optimist behind these upbeat plays. A young man, full of fun and *joie de vivre*, who understood the love and lust of other young men in the prime of life, their banter and crude jokes, but also their hopes and aspirations. However, he also understood the feelings of women, their flirtatiousness, their vulnerability, their sense of fairness and their surer instincts about deep emotions. Did Will Shakespeare love all women and enjoy talking to them whenever he could? Probably. How else would he have been able to invent such plausible female characters and to identify so closely with them? He couldn't have been a man who was ill at ease with women, only comfortable with masculine conversation: many Elizabethan men must have envied his rare gift!

His history plays showed the playgoers a very different side, as they do us today. He had an unerring grasp of politics, of the way things work at court, amongst royalty and nobility, in other words, those who controlled everything, at home and abroad. He was fascinated by power, how it was won and lost, used and abused: he understood wars and battles, crimes and Machiavellian scheming, the plots and counter-plots which were so much part of his times, and had been throughout a succession of monarchies. His dramatist's brain could impose order and structure on events of the past, isolating the most important, recognising cause and effect, and above all, fleshing out the key protagonists so that their actions revealed motivation and were highly plausible to the audience watching. Only Will, out of all the playwrights, showed this degree of psychological insight, a perception which was to become more and more acute, culminating in the great tragic heroes he created towards the end of his career. Far from naïve, he had no illusions about human beings and the depths to which they could descend to achieve their ends. His own instinctive sense of right and wrong meant that the versions of history he created showed the whole picture, the gamut of virtues and vices, the consequences of acts for all time. He wasn't an overt moralist, preferring to direct his audience, subtly. His serious speeches throw out a challenge for the individual to react: what do *you* think? How would you judge this person? Make up your *own* mind about this!

Those who knew him best, his company of actors, must have recognised in Will someone who was both a hard worker *and* multi-talented; an outsider originally, he'd become one of the key members of the group as an actor, theatre-manager and chief writer. As his writing success grew, he didn't become separate from the group but continued to take small parts on stage for many years, so was very much part of the team. This suggests a natural modesty and an ability to get on with the others, as well as an enjoyment of what he was doing, acting and directing. He was probably able to get the best out of the fellow actors he knew so well. It wouldn't all be plain sailing and there's evidence that the company had a disagreement with comedian, Will Kempe, who left them towards the end of the century.

It's likely, however, that many of the company were close friends, especially, Richard Burbage. Over the years there must have been a kind of symbiotic relationship between the two, as Will created more and more leading characters for Richard to immortalise on stage. Then there were the two actors, Hemminge and Condell, who, through their friendship, carried out an invaluable service to Will's memory by publishing the plays after his death.

The adjective *gentle* was often used to describe Will, by people who knew him, implying not merely softness of manner and kindness, but courtesy, fairness and integrity – the virtues of true gentility, from where we get the term *gentle*man and all its associations. Whether Will also sulked or got impatient with others, or lost his temper if they mangled his words, we'll never know, but we'd like to imagine that most differences were overcome in the comradeship of the alehouse. The *Lord Chamberlain's Men* needed to get along together – their success depended on it.

For all his reported affability, Will wasn't naïve. He must have been street-wise, as we'd say today: sensitive to public moods, aware of the latest gossip and fashions, of what was hot, and what was not. Who's in, who's out. His plays show that he understood the way the world wagged. London was his element and he must have soaked up everything happening around him. He could hold his own in courts and palaces, smoothing the way to success. The *Lord Chamberlain's Men* were fast becoming stars of the entertainment world but they had to remember their place in the court hierarchy where they were, in effect, paid servants. They had to behave with deference and elaborate courtesy to fit in at court and would inevitably encounter some condescension and snobbery as the norm. Many of the courtiers would, like as not, look down on Will as a low-born countryman and a mere player, but I suspect the more intuitive ones would discern the fierce intellect beneath the gracious exterior, respecting the person he was, rather than where he came from.

But what made him tick? Did anyone, even those close to him, really know what was in his heart?

As the century drew to a close, Will was becoming an expert at his art, no doubt about it; he could now have answered Robert Greene's taunt by saying that far from being a mere jack-of-all-trades, he had become a very proficient master of one: writing successful plays for the stage, with histories and comedies his particular speciality. You have to imagine the adrenaline-rush of the writer's creative process, *together with* that of the actor's live performance. Will knew both and must have experienced them time and time again. After the uncertainty of the years in Stratford, or wherever else he'd lived on the way to fame, he had found his place in life, totally immersed in the world of the theatre.

6. Enter Ben Jonson

He was indeed honest, and of an open and free nature, had an excellent fantasy, brave notions and gentle expressions.

This is Ben Jonson writing about Will after his death, though he wasn't always so complimentary when his friend was alive.

It's difficult to discuss the real Will Shakespeare with any certainty, but it might be helpful to compare him with fellow playwright, Ben Jonson, who was a very different kind of character.

Ben, with whom Will had a prickly but lasting friendship, was a large, aggressive and quarrelsome man who was always getting himself into fights and worse. He had a similar background to Will and was proud of his classical education by way of a scholarship to Westminster School. After being apprenticed to his step-father as a bricklayer – which he hated, both the job and the man – he soon found his way into the world of the theatre and play-writing, one of his specialities being black comedies which grimly personified and satirised the worst characteristics of humankind. They were very different from Will's upbeat comedies which show a basic belief in human good, a kind of covert moral message, that *all shall be well and all manner of thing shall be well,* to use the words of the 15th century anchorite, Julian of Norwich. For the deserving characters, that is. The undeserving usually got their come-uppance or m*easure for measure,* a nifty phrase which Will used as the title for one of his darker comedies.

In one of his fights Ben killed a man and was sentenced to be hanged, but managed to escape the gallows by a legal loophole. He was able to recite the liturgy in Latin – the so called *neck verses* because they saved your neck! This was seen as proof that he had studied Divinity (he hadn't) and saved him from execution – the best argument I've ever come across for studying a dead language like Latin. He was reprieved and branded on his thumb with a T for Tyburn, (where executions took place), a final warning that there would be no let-off next time.

Words were the currency of both men. It's said that Will did Ben a favour and took one of his plays for performance by the Lord Chamberlain's Men, leading to an ongoing relationship which was probably a vibrant mix of warm friendship and professional respect, interspersed with some periods of discord and animosity. Like Will, Ben had been an actor, too, briefly, but soon abandoned it in favour of writing and seeking patronage in high places; Will, as you know, addressed his lucrative narrative poems to his patron, Southampton, but preferred to return to play-writing and total involvement in the theatre. Ben was more interested in actively progressing his career as a published writer, and oversaw more publications of his plays than Will ever did; Ben, though he behaved rashly at times, gave more thought to the enduring nature of his work and his fame, or so it seems from reliable evidence. Though outwardly more rebellious, later in his career Ben was to conform, concentrating more on what the court and public wanted, for example creating elaborately-staged shows called masques which were all the rage for a time with the Jacobeans. Ultimately, I think Will was the more subversive of the two, though contemporaries probably didn't always recognise how strong this trait was in the seemingly genial actor-dramatist.

We have written evidence, from various sources, of Ben's caustic jibes at his friend's expense, but also of his great respect and strong affection for Will: in the preface to the Folio edition of Will's plays, published after his death, Ben wrote, eulogising his friend, *He was not of an age but for all time,* the most astonishingly far-sighted prediction about anyone that I've ever heard, as well as being an endorsement of Shakespeare's genius.

If you read some of the witticisms he made at Will's expense during his lifetime, it's easy to conclude, without being a trained psychologist, that Ben was sometimes jealous of Will's success, probably envying his imagination, his facility with words and his flexibility of thought. Will had an empathy with his fellow men – and women – which must have bemused Ben, who was often cynical and intolerant, seeing the worst in his fellows. He would recognise the voice of compassion which ran through Will's work, for all the comic high jinks, and he knew his friend well enough to appreciate the characteristics which ran counter to his own fiery personality. For example, Will must have behaved with a level-headedness which Ben could never have managed in a month of compulsory church-going Sundays!

Methinks Ben probably understood him better than most, well enough to know that Will had a dark side, just as he, himself, did; after all, Will had already written *Richard III,* and was to go on to write the late great tragedies, giving the world villains, such as Iago and Claudius, not to mention complex, vulnerable protagonists like Macbeth and Hamlet. How these plays must have amazed contemporaries who had him down as a master of comedies and histories! Not always the *sweet swan of Avon,* Will was to expose evil and to show the suffering of mankind in a totally different way from Ben. Will's way. The two playwrights were poles apart in temperament, but they were allies, they understood each other, even if they came at arguments from different sides and indulged in tournaments of wit with feints and thrusts, just for the hell of it.

Risk averse

Unlike Ben, Will seems to have avoided trouble and scandal throughout most of his London career, when many about him seemed to court it or become accidentally embroiled.

All Elizabethans lived lives much closer to death than we can imagine today. London was a mad, bad world to stay alive in. Apart from the plague, there were countless incurable illnesses, like the *sweating sickness,* which could carry you off quickly: you could be perfectly healthy in the morning and dead by nightfall. No wonder recklessness set in. *Eat, drink and be merry for tomorrow ye die,* had a literal significance most of us are lucky enough to be able to ignore today. Life was cheap. People lived it to the full, especially the young testosterone-fuelled men of whom there were many. Old people were in the minority. Most men carried a weapon, usually a sword, and Will almost certainly would have done most of the time – his sword is one of the items mentioned in his will. How easy then for a disagreement to escalate out of control and end up in a fight, fatal for one or more involved, like the one in the play where Romeo kills Tybalt in a street brawl.

Add alcohol to the potent mix of young blood, anger and adrenalin, and, as you know, more violence is triggered. Nearly everyone drank in England, even the poor. Ale of various strengths was brewed as the main way of assuaging thirst because the water wasn't safe to drink. Apart from milk and some herbal drinks, there was little choice – no tea or coffee yet. Children were practically weaned on *small* beer as it was called. Most people would have had some ale by breakfast time and would continue to drink at mealtimes throughout the day; these were the moderate drinkers! The serious ones must have been completely legless by lunchtime. Will, according to one of the popular versions of his character, was a hard-drinker and, according to one source, over-indulgence with friends led to his death.

A lot of men came to an untimely end through being *splenetive and rash,* to quote Will again. The spleen was seen as the organ responsible for anger and bile. Human biology at the time saw the body as comprising a mix of fluids, called *humours,* which determined your temperament; if you were *choleric* by nature, like Ben, your blood was up most of the time, often leading to a fatal lack of self-control. In spite of his probable fondness for a drink, Will seems to have developed an instinct for self-preservation, perhaps as part of the double life he led, learning to rein in feelings and to avoid extremes of behaviour or alcoholic excess. He was a survivor. He kept his head – literally – at a time when others about him were losing theirs. He would have known some of those who were executed at the Queen's command: friends, acquaintances, courtiers, noblemen and women, distant Catholic relatives from the Arden family who went to their deaths for religious and political crimes, often after they'd been stretched on the rack to make them confess, whether they were guilty or not.

The systems for torture were extremely sophisticated. The Queen's spymaster, Sir Francis Walsingham, had been feared throughout the land, with his network of informers, and he was obsessive about carrying out his duties to Elizabeth. On his deathbed he was reported as saying: *would that I had served my God as I have served my Queen.* How much did he have on his conscience, I wonder.

His successor, Lord Burghley's son, who had his own private torture chamber, was made in the same mould. So, too, was Richard Topcliffe, Elizabeth's inquisitor, who was psychopathic in his desire to extract confessions. Even if victims escaped with their lives, they were often so broken in health, like the playwright Thomas Kydd, that they didn't live long after interrogation.

Will, as a playwright and actor, was often at court, close to the Queen, and therefore had to be careful and discreet: plays were often seen as vehicles for sedition, reaching a wide audience, as they did. For example, speeches in them might contain cryptic messages, or the storyline could invite comparison with a contemporary political situation and implicitly criticise those in power. However, apart from one occasion, Will seems to have avoided giving offence, unlike some of his fellow playwrights. Either he was extremely canny at concealing subversive text or he was innately *circumspect,* a word which means, literally, *seeing around,* and by implication, not taking sides or getting involved. Probably he was both. And perhaps he was naturally ambivalent about many of the political and religious matters of his day, preferring to use a wide-angled lens to see and show what happened when the time was *out of joint,* when something was rotten in the state.

Had Will learnt to be cautious at a young age after the pain of his father's disgrace and his own enforced marriage? Or from the brutal reprisals meted out to his distant Catholic relatives? How much was he repressing, bottling up inside him in the years following his *salad days* when he was *green in judgment*? At the time when he was becoming successful, he seems to have remained level-headed, avoiding resentment from others and refusing to get involved in some of the wilder exploits of contemporary playwrights. Being alert to the clear and present dangers of his life shows remarkable astuteness and maturity, a steady, sure-footed way of proceeding down the path of his life.

Perhaps he had to tread carefully because of his family's concealed, or barely concealed, Catholicism. As far as we know he was never arrested or interrogated about his religion. Either he hid his family's religion, dissociating himself totally from the Ardens, or perhaps he was a *safe* Catholic i.e. *not* fervent about his faith and certainly not a member of any radicalised groups. Perhaps he was protected by the Queen, as some of her favourite noblemen were, along with Catholics, like the musician, Thomas Byrd, who *was* interrogated but then left alone. I find it strange, now more has emerged about the Shakespeare family religion, that Will seems to have been given unlimited access to the court, carte blanche to perform before Queen Elizabeth and later King James. Some researchers have suggested he was, in private, a practising Catholic, but would he have remained undetected by Elizabeth's spy network? Unlikely. I think it's much more likely that he had safely distanced himself from his family's religious background.

7. Sex and the City

As well as keeping out of trouble, Will seems to have avoided a reputation for loose living or being implicated in any of the sex scandals of the sort which were very common at court, the perpetrators often losing royal favour as a result. Will's work couldn't have left him much time for a private life – by which we usually mean a love-life/sex-life – or could it? Where there's a will there's a way! Behind the public façade, Will, seems to have been good at keeping his private life private. Experts can tell you where he lodged in London with precise addresses, even who his near neighbours were and which were the likely pubs he frequented, but on a more personal level, it's mainly guesswork. And, as usual, there is a whole raft of possibilities, not to mention contradictory ones, of course.

The duality of Will's life continued: no one knows how often he went back to the home fire to see his family. About once a year, is the usual guestimate, perhaps during the weeks of Lent when the theatres were shut, leading up to Holy Week and Easter. He was possibly quite another person back in Warwickshire with his family and friends. We all tend to play different roles, often without realising we're doing it. Few of the residents of Stratford would have much idea of the London life of a group of players, let alone the life of their chief writer, though they would have heard of the growing popularity of the new theatres and the must-see plays, and may well have associated Will with a certain raffish glamour. He was the local lad who had made good in the big city, but not all would have approved of his lifestyle. There were growing numbers of Puritans in Stratford by this time and they would almost certainly have viewed him as immoral. An actor *and* a poet? Clearly a sinner beyond redemption!

At least when Will journeyed back home, he could take a break from the pressure of work, but there could have been stresses of a different sort. Perhaps he always felt he'd let the family down – we'll never know – though he gave them back their financial stability and respectability. Quality time, as we call it, with his family, might come at a different sort of price, and would depend on his relationship with Anne, with his children – and with his ageing parents.

Love cheat?

As far as we know, there were no more children born to Anne and Will. Was he faithful to the four-poster marriage bed, to become famous in his last will and testament? Probably not. I think it's rather unlikely that he led a totally celibate life in London, given the nature of the entertainment industry and the fact that he wrote some rather juicy sonnets about love and sex. Players were notorious for loose living, and there must have been loads of available women in the taverns and brothels around the theatre areas, often plying their trade amongst the audiences. Though, in fact, most of the members of *The Lord Chamberlain's Men* were married with homes and families close by which gives the lie to the public perception at the time of all actors being promiscuous and lawless. There was no reason why Will could not have brought Anne and the children down to London; he could by now have afforded more expensive lodgings, but there is no evidence that he did and most of the known houses he lived in were modest rented rooms.

As often happens with Will's story, there are conflicting accounts. On the one hand there are valid-sounding comments by contemporaries to the effect that Will didn't do *debauchery,* by which they meant going to brothels and generally sleeping around. The d-word was a strongly pejorative one in those days, carrying with it all the disapproval of loose living, but also all the associations of the consequences, like STDs, especially syphilis, which was rife in Elizabethan times and for which there was no certain cure. Too much sex could seriously damage your health in those days.

On the other hand, there is a Jack-the-lad type story of Will having a one-night stand with a woman theatre-goer, a sort of Elizabethan *groupie*! She was originally propositioned by Richard Burbage, who was playing the title role in *Richard III*, but, when he knocked on her door, after the show, he found Will had got there first:

Upon a time when Burbage played Richard III there was a citizen grew so far in liking with him that before she went from the play she appointed him to come that night unto her by the name of Richard III. Shakespeare, overhearing the conclusion, went before, was entertained and at his game ere Burbage came. Then, message being brought that Richard III was at the door, Shakespeare caused return to be made that William the Conqueror was before Richard III.

This tale of seduction and wit, of which even James Bond would be a tad jealous, was told in the diary of a London lawyer who had seen the play and heard the anecdote.

The Mystery of the Sonnets

If the sonnets, which range widely in mood, are more personal than anything else Will ever wrote – and I think they are – no can agree on their content and what he is actually *sharing* with us, though experts have agonised for years. Some are well known: many are a difficult read. Are they for real or not? Did Will have a mistress for some or most of the time he was in London? A dark-haired and possibly dark-skinned, woman whom he addresses in the sonnets? Did he have a series of infatuations, one of which may have been a homosexual love affair with an attractive young man, unidentified, like the lady? Trust Will to write his sonnets to a fair lord and a dark lady… did he invent the contrast? Was it all an elaborate fiction?

This next section has caused me a few headaches in the writing and it's certainly longer than intended. I need a goodly draught of Rhenish…

Will wrote 154 sonnets, (from the Italian meaning *little song*), probably over a number of years, if we think of the one to Anne Hathaway, though many have been dated to the last decade of the 16th century. There are computer programs now which can date Will's writing according to the lexical groups he favours at specific times.

Apart from a few pirated versions, they weren't published till 1609, though they were probably doing the rounds among small groups of his friends as they were written. That was the point of sonnets really – they were private, personal poems, the structure and form of them coming from, guess where, Italy! They were concise, having only 14 lines, and lent themselves perfectly to the subject of love. The fashion for writing a sonnet to the woman of your dreams as part of the courtship ritual came from Italy too, and had caught on big time. There must have been vast numbers of bad sonnets by Elizabethan lovers, full of genuine yearning, or just pretending to be, composed because it was *de rigeur*. There's no doubt that at times Will mocks the *dying for love* clichés which were current, but at other times his own emotions feel very raw.

On the one hand, Will may not have wanted his sonnets published at all and may have been mortified by them when they were leaked to a printer; they may not have had the global reach of *Facebook,* but they would definitely have similar potential for embarrassing the writer. On the other hand, he may have been quite comfortable with their being in the public domain: many are so cryptic, anyway, that perhaps he wasn't too worried about people understanding them.

But, and it's a big *but,* many of them shout pain and suffering so clearly that you can't ignore them, though critics did for centuries, or dismiss them as fashionable satire. They are full of witty conceits, in-jokes and wordplay, conundrums in themselves, but they also speak so eloquently of the different moods of love, including jealousy. Will knew the power of poetry to transcend time, a common theme in the sonnets, whereas, ironically, he probably saw his plays as a much more transient art form, a bit like television today.

But I keep coming back to the puzzle of publication. If Will had learnt the hard way from the events surrounding his marriage to be circumspect about his love life, why did he publish his sonnets? As usual with Will-puzzles, there are polar-opposite answers, together with any number of options in between. They were the most famous love poems in the world:

- Written as poetic exercises and as fictitious as the plays?

- Highly personal autobiographical poetry, a conduit for Will's feelings about actual relationships.

- A mix of both.

It's anybody's guess!

If you believe the first or second theories when you read these extraordinary poems, I think it's reasonable to infer that Anne, his wife, was no longer the love of Will's life, if she ever had been. Nor was she the inspirational muse behind them.

One of the main difficulties with the sonnets is that some of the most beautiful and best known are written to a man. This worries modern readers far less than it would have done at one time, but it does raise the whole question of whether Will was bisexual or at least bi-curious. Opinion has swung from complete denial of any homoerotic content to the other extreme, with scholars also mining all the plays for possible gay innuendo and evidence of homosexual relationships. It's possible to argue that some of the male friendships, like the one between Antonio and Bassanio in *The Merchant of Venice, could* be homosexual, in that Antonio loses his lover to Portia, if you want to construe it that way, though none comes anywhere near the suggestiveness of the relationship between the King, and Piers Gaveston, in Marlowe's *Edward II.*

You need to know that the word *love* was used rather differently in Will's time, having wide connotations, just as it does today, but being used much more openly between men to denote a strong friendship bond, *not* necessarily sexual in nature. This kind of ardour in masculine friendship is less familiar today and can frequently lead to classroom giggles when students are reading Shakespeare. Though, perhaps in the more touchy-feely western world, now, we are returning to this very friendly, familiar use of the word *love*, which is always undergoing semantic change? The advent of text messages has brought a rash of kisses and heart symbols, not to mention the cuddly *lol* and *luvu* being used copiously…by the guys, too, as they get in touch with their feminine side and become less self-conscious about man-hugs!

I think Elizabethan men *were* more in touch with their feminine side –you've only got to look at the clothes… Yes, the male figure was emphasized, with broad shoulders, narrow waists, tights and codpieces, but outfits of well-to-do men also included frills and feathered hats, exaggerated ruffs, luscious fabrics like lace and velvet, not to mention vast amounts of bling! They were definitely peacocks strutting their stuff and they spent a fortune on clothes. It was a full-on age, ostentation and excess being the way to go if you could afford it.

It's unclear how different sexual orientation and relationships were regarded by the Elizabethans – we don't really know. Sodomy was a crime in Elizabethan England, but not one which seems to have been prosecuted much, though religion taught that it was a sin against God, as was incest, one of the trumped up charges against Anne Boleyn which led to her (and her brother's) execution.

A young man's beauty was often praised quite openly, as it is in Will's sonnets. In tone the first poems start out more like the respectful salutations to the Earl of Southampton, with which Will prefaced *Venus* and *Adonis* and *The Rape of Lucrece* – indeed, they *could well* be addressed to Southampton as part of the patron-poet relationship, as Will exhorts him to marry and have children who will continue his line and reproduce the physical beauty of their father. Southampton was an attractive, rather effeminate-looking young man and it's quite possible that Will's feelings for him went beyond friendship. Or not.

The strange and confusingly ungrammatical dedication to *Mr WH* has caused an avalanche of books and papers to be written on the subject by literary sleuths expounding many theories over the years. Was Mr W.H. a Lord or, as the dedication suggests, a commoner? Perhaps he was an actor? If they are addressed to the Earl of Southampton, Henry Wriothsley, did Will switch the initials round? And call him plain *Mister* to confuse people? Perhaps Will was strongly attracted to another young man, like the 18 year-old nobleman, William Herbert, who has been suggested as a possible candidate with the right initials. By God's holy teeth, Will, you'd be amazed how many have tried to solve this mystery over the years! But, then, as Anthony Holden plausibly suggests, if the sonnets were published without Will's knowledge, then the publisher probably wrote the dedication, and *not* Will at all!

The poems written to *his dark mistress* are more down-to-earth in language and sentiment: Will *includes sexual content*, as they say in the film and TV warnings. He also deliberately flouts the romantic conventions of the sonnet tradition, mocking the stereotype of the young man about to expire for love. He ridicules some of the standard clichés and the way the women in poems are idealised, possessed of beauty which is always of the fair-haired, fair-skinned, blue-eyed type:

My mistress' eyes are nothing like the sun; ....

......If snow be white, why then her breasts are dun;

If Will's lady was real – and I think she was, for the sonnets seem to go much deeper than superficial satire – she was dark in colouring and could have been Portuguese, Italian, even a negress. As well as turning the idea of conventional beauty on its head, Will seems to relish the ethno-erotic qualities of the woman he loves. Various potential lovers have been suggested by researchers for the identity of this woman – *cherchez la femme* this time – from prostitutes to nobly born women. There have even been attempts to open up a grave and disinter the body of one likely suspect, Mary Fitton, a maid of honour of the Queen, to see if there are copies of sonnets buried with her that would confirm her identification as Will's mistress.

I think it's safe to conclude that Will was very sensitive to beauty of all kinds and that he *understood* and could empathise with a wide variety of sexual feelings and relationships: one or more of the mysteries of Will's love life could well be locked in the lines of these sonnets. It's also possible that they were much clearer to Will's contemporaries – the Elizabethans revelled in riddles after all – but somehow I doubt it. Perhaps even close friends didn't know the identities of the fair lord and the dark lady. If, of course, they existed.

Meanwhile, something cruel was waiting backstage for Will. Or deep in the pit underneath the stage. Something which would rock the most stable foundations of his life to the core.

8. My absent child

In August 1596, the church register of Holy Trinity in Stratford records the death of Hamnet, son of William Shakespeare. He was eleven. No one knows why Hamnet died – it could have been the plague or some other fatal sickness. It's unlikely that Will was at home when he died. He may not have made it back in time for the funeral either, though he probably went home to comfort the family and share in their grief. Did the sadness of losing his only son, one half of the pair of boy/girl twins, bring him close to Anne or did it cause a breach that could not be healed? We will never know because as usual there are no personal documents, only the stark statement of the parish register and some oft-quoted lines in Will's play, *King John*:

Grief fills the room up of my absent child,

Lies in his bed, walks up and down with me,

Puts on his pretty looks, repeats his words...

All we can do is bring our own experience of loss to bear or to try and imagine the reality of Will's grief for his son and its consequences, even though it was an age when children died frequently. Will had his work, his life in London, his second family, the company of actors, to give him some stability, but the part of his life which he'd probably taken for granted had suddenly changed for all time. What he had perhaps felt as a dull pain, his separation from family in Stratford, must have been made *sharper than a serpent's tooth* by the death of Hamnet. If he still harboured feelings of guilt about his move to London, then these, too, must have been exacerbated by what was a cruel turn of events. Just when everything had seemed gilded with success in London, the more stable, secure part of his double life, represented by Stratford, had proved vulnerable beyond belief.

Vulnerability was perhaps part of the motivation for two actions Will took next, along with a desire to do something tangible for the family. Only nine months after Hamnet's death, Will bought a large house in Stratford – you can still see where it stood today – for his family to live in, and over the next few years acquired other property and land back home, as if to reclaim his roots and reassert his sense of belonging to Warwickshire. Was he making a bid for permanence and security, trying to shore up the damage done to everything he held dear? Even though he perhaps hadn't realised before just how dear it all was to him.

New Place, itself, required some literal shoring up and damage limitation. Though it was a grand house, one of the largest in Stratford, it was dilapidated, *needing work,* as the estate agent's euphemism goes today. Will got it at a bargain price and renovated it gradually – he was canny with money and not one to fritter away new wealth. Was there a part of him which enjoyed the prestige and status of this new house, which his family could certainly not have afforded in the past? Was he proud to return home, knowing he had made good and restored his father's fortunes? Did he feel he had wiped away former indiscretions, his father's and his own? Or were all these achievements overshadowed by Hamnet's death, soured by sadness?

Even before the purchase of *New Place*, just ten weeks after his child's death, Will decided to reapply for a family coat of arms so that his father could be given the title of *Gentleman.* This time, twenty years after John's first application, the family were successful, on the basis of their ancestral line and the fact that Will's father was respectable and solvent again. A coat of arms was drawn up with a simple spear design and a motto, *Not without Right*, as if to proudly assert their credentials as a family. John Shakespeare had made it from farm labourer to gentleman in the space of fifty years. But perhaps it wasn't just about John. Comments about Will which have come down to us emphasize his likeability, his equanimity, his innate courtesy, as if he was a man without *side*, as we would say today, but for all that he must have had an awareness of his humble origins compared with high-born people he met every day. It would be difficult not to in the Elizabethan hierarchical society. The house and the coat of arms were undoubtedly status symbols for Will and probably those close to him knew just how much they meant to him privately – friends like Ben Jonson who was shrewd enough to understand what lay beneath the modest exterior that Will presented to the world.

Ironically, his dad, John, did not enjoy the prestige of his own coat of arms for very long, as he died in 1601 (another funeral and trip to Stratford). The rights to the title, shield and blazon passed to Will, who now had no son of his own to inherit them and keep them for the posterity of the Shakespeare family.

What sort of emotional state was Will in after the death of Hamnet? How did he cope with his grief? Did he weep partly out of love, partly out of anger, partly out of guilt? Most people who've suffered grief will speak of a maelstrom of different, sometimes conflicting, emotions as being part of one of the worst experiences of the human condition. Will had been raised by parents, who grew up in a Catholic England, so it's possible that guilt from the old religion was telling him that in some way he was being punished: he'd been a bad husband and now his son was dead. *He wasn't there for him*, as the modern jargon has it. *My grief lies onward and my joy behind,* he writes in one of his sonnets.

In his play, *Hamlet,* there is a lucid description of depression and suicidal feelings, which many of us will recognise as being wholly accurate in its depiction of the sense of the utter pointlessness of life:

O God! O God!

How weary, stale, flat and unprofitable

Seem to me all the uses of this world!

If Will felt like this after his son's death, one thing that is known is that he continued to work, in spite of such an emotional watershed – or perhaps because of it. Key plays like *The Merchant of Venice, As You Like it, Henry V, Julius Caesar* and *Hamlet* were written sometime in the years immediately following Hamnet's death, the last four probably all in one prolific year, 1599. You can't get much more of a varied selection than these: two comedies, an English history, a Roman tragi-history, and *Hamlet,* perhaps the greatest of the tragedies.

Will kept up the momentum: he'd been writing and working in the theatre for nigh on a decade. There were more playwrights out there now, even a kind of *war of the poets,* as it was called, in which the different writers became highly competitive, making nasty jibes about each other within the scripts of their plays. It looks as if Will stayed out of this, for the most part, though he may have joined in from time to time, probably having a pop at Ben! The university v. non-university rivalry seems to have continued, too: a line in a contemporary play shows how well known Will had become:

Few of the university men pen plaies well, they smell too much of that writer, Ovid... Why, here's our fellow Shakespeare puts them all down...

Whoever wrote this – and we don't know who it was – showed a remarkable sensitivity to *our fellow, Shakespeare's* special qualities as a popular writer, compared with the university men. Will had displayed wit over and over, proved again and again that he could write with passion, tell a good tale, create vital characters... also that he possessed the common touch which made his plays into show-stoppers. But there was more to come: a growing sense of purpose, perhaps a wish to do something good with his art, which was already starting to define him and set him apart, as it came to fruition in the fathomless reaches of his mind.

Breaking News

In 1599 *The Lord Chamberlain's Men* finally got their own theatre, a permanent home for their performances. *The Globe* was wonderfully named, for globes had only just begun to be made and were prized objects, showing the whole of planet earth so people could visualize it in a way they never had before. Each of the new theatres *was* a whole world in itself, but *The Globe* was a particularly fine example with its huge apron stage, two tall marbled pillars which held up the roof over the stage, the underside of which was painted with clouds to represent the sky, called, for obvious reasons, *the heavens.* Over the doors of the theatre were the words *sia Totus mundus agit histrionem,* or *the whole world plays the actor.*

Will often used the theatre as metaphor for the world and compared a man's life to a play being performed on stage, as, for example, in the following well-known speech from *As You Like It:*

All the world's a stage

And all the men and women merely players.

They have their exits and their entrances

And one man in his time plays many parts,

His acts being seven ages.

You can visit the replica *Globe* today on the South Bank, not far from where the original stood, though it's smaller than Will's *Globe,* but authentic in detail and design. You can watch a play there, seated or standing, and book a tour when there's no performance taking place.

There's a good story about how the original *Globe* came into existence: the lease on *The Theatre* in Shoreditch, where the Lord Chamberlain's Men often acted, was about to expire, but Shakespeare and Co found a legal anomaly which said that they owned the building though not the land. With considerable enterprise, they decided to re-site the whole structure. They hired workmen to help them dismantle the theatre in the dead of night, and transported it, bit by bit, across the Thames to Bankside, where it was slowly rebuilt. Recycling is nothing new!

A famous period in the history of drama followed. The best acting company, with the best resident-writer, now had the best theatre, giving them total control over their repertoire and all aspects of their business. Many plays were staged at *The Globe* over the years, mainly Will's, but sometimes those of other writers. It's thought that the first play performed there was *Julius Caesar,* put on in that famous year, 1599, when Will was thirty-five.

Losing the Plot

Two years later, in 1601, *The Lord Chamberlain's Men* nearly jeopardised their successful career by becoming, wittingly or unwittingly, involved in the last conspiracy of Elizabeth's reign. Her one-time favourite and toy-boy, the Earl of Essex, had messed up badly on an expedition to Ireland and had fallen from favour. In what seems like a totally unhinged act of retaliation, he rode into London with a small force of men, bent upon seizing the throne, and hoping people would rally to the Catholic cause. No one did. The night before the planned coup, The Lord Chamberlain's Men had been persuaded, and paid well, to put on a performance of Will's play, *Richard II,* from one of the cycles of history plays. They were to include the deposition scene, usually banned, where the rightful king has to hand over his crown to the usurper, Bolingbroke, who became King Henry IV. Presumably Essex identified himself with Bolingbroke and was using the play as an example of a successful coup to win support for his own attempt on the throne.

What was Will thinking of? Was he feeling suicidal? He and the other players must have been mad to agree to do this scene which had never before been staged in front of the Queen, so sensitive was the material. Elizabeth got the point all right: *I am Richard II. Know ye not that?* she is reported to have said.

Amazingly, however, the company got away with it, pleading, in their defence, that they had been tricked and manipulated. A likely story, but then they were actors! Will's illustrious career could have ended at Tyburn tree, i.e. the gallows, with many of his major plays unwritten. Essex and his supporters weren't so lucky; they were arrested and executed, but the Queen's favourite acting company escaped with their lives.

On the stage of history, the Queen's life was drawing to a close, which makes Essex's rebellion look even more foolish. But hindsight is a wonderful thing.

Artist's impression of the construction of the original Globe Theatre, built 1599, destroyed by fire in 1613, rebuilt 1614 and closed down in 1642.

INTERLUDE

Will's skills

Just for a bit of fun I've written an imaginary CV and a personality profile for the Immortal Bard:

Name: William Shakespeare

D.o.b. 23.04.1564

Education: King's New Grammar School, Stratford-on-Avon

Subjects studied: Latin, classical literature, grammar, rhetoric, argument and poetic form. Divinity and Bible Study.

Interests: Writing and acting. Reading plays, stories, myths and legends, histories and chronicles. Studying accounts of exploration, sea voyages, scientific development, astronomy, architecture. Listening to music – instrumental composition and songs. Reading in original Latin, French and Italian, as well as in translation.

Skill levels: High degree of literacy and good communication skills. Strong financial acumen.

Early Work Experience: in the leather and glove-making trades: also as a private tutor.

Recent Career: travelling actor and player in the London theatre. Published poet with dedications to *My Lord, the Earl of Southampton*. Actor, chief play-maker and sharer for *The Lord Chamberlain's Men*, thereafter *The King's Men*, with accredited performances at *The Globe Theatre* and *The Blackfriars Theatre* (part owner of both theatres) and before their Majesties, Queen Elizabeth I and King James I, of England and Great Britannia.

Personal traits: self-confidence, drive and determination. Calmness in a crisis and resourcefulness. Loyalty and reliability. Good leadership and people skills. Ability to work well as a team member but also to act independently and make decisions. Creativity and originality.

Personality profile of Will Shakespeare

I've tried to unlock Will's character, using Cattell's 16 factor personality model, still employed in universities and businesses, and to imagine what Will might score were he doing the questionnaire today. The test is based on 16 constructs describing personality and a standardized score between 1 and 10, low to high, is given for each one to achieve an overall profile. Some of the original descriptors were later dropped from the test by psychologists, hence the non-consecutive lettering of the list.

A. Warmth: Score 8/9

It seems a no-brainer to give Will high marks here, as someone who must have not merely liked people, but been utterly fascinated by them. He must have been a friendly guy who got close to people and encouraged them to open up to him. Look at the extraordinary range of characters in his plays, both men and women, who are so believable. Part of the realism of his characterisation has to come from his empathy *with* them, his compassionate treatment *of* them, his ability to understand both the good and bad *in* them.

In addition to creating such credible people, Will's own lifestyle was predicated on the social base of the theatre and the company of actors; he could not have worked the way he did, day in day out, in close proximity to his colleagues, without getting on with them and being liked by them. That's not to say he was always equable and even-tempered – who is? But they all relied upon each other for their livelihood and existence. In his unique place at the epicentre of the theatre business, Will must have been out-going, a good communicator, as we would say today, and able to put across his ideas without being over-bearing. This seems to be borne out by the fact that the adjective *gentle* is used frequently about Will in documents by contemporaries and it's easy to imagine that he was a warm-hearted and sympathetic person who would achieve a high score for this first personality descriptor.

However, my feeling is that Will is not someone who *always* needs company – writers by their very nature are detached and have to work alone much of the time. Perhaps, as I've speculated before, there was a reserve about Will, a feeling that he didn't give much away about himself. This is hinted at in *Brief Lives*, by Aubrey, who says, in rather contradictory fashion, that Will was *good company*, but was *not a company keeper*. What are we to make of this? Aubrey was writing in the late 1600s, so would not have known Will, but he would have talked to people who *had* known him, for example, William Davenant. (More about this other William later.)

B. Reasoning: Score 10

Being highly intelligent and a fast learner, Will must be at the top of the scale here. He would have a high IQ, if such tests were available in the 16th century. He read widely, understood Latin, a rational, inflected language, and most likely had a good grasp of modern languages like Italian and French, which he probably taught himself. The plots and sub-plots of his plays are often complex, intricate and interwoven, compared with those by contemporary playwrights. Of course there are some flaws – he was creating material for a few hours' traffic on the stage, a pretty transient art form; he didn't know that his plays would be still be closely studied in four hundred years! In many plays, especially the histories, he shows a highly perceptive understanding of power struggles at the top levels of society, of the world of politics and the corridors of power. He was definitely capable of abstract and complex thinking.

C. Emotional stability: Score 7

Will shows an insight into emotional *in*stability that is way ahead of his time, but what was he like, himself, with regard to dealing with his own feelings? In the plays he shows sensitivity towards a complete range of emotions in his characters, especially in the tragedies, which encompass the worst kind of events that can happen in life. His characters cope – or they don't. Will may have teetered on the brink of despair, himself, as he understands so well the vulnerability of the mind to breakdown. But – and it's a big *but* – what we know of his life and lifestyle indicates a maturity in Will and an ability to face reality, to say *we are where we are*. He's too sane to lose his marbles, in spite of personal tragedy.

It's often said that genius does not deal well with the realities of day to day life, but it seems to me that Will has a toughness all his own. He's a fighter. Perhaps he's learnt coping stratagems, as we'd say today. Perhaps he's taught himself a calmness and control, to match the resilience he's inherited from his father. Perhaps his family in Stratford have contributed to his emotional stability – he returns to them throughout his life – and when in London he has his surrogate family of actors around him to keep him grounded. He must play, and maintain, a responsible role with both these close-knit groups. (I'm trying to avoid using that over-worked word, *caring*, to describe the Immortal Bard.)

E. Dominance: Score 7

This is a difficult one and I've already spent some time contrasting Will with his friend, Ben Jonson, who seems to me much more of an aggressive, impulsive alpha male. But Will must have been confident and assertive in his own way to have made his career in a tough world and to have achieved such success in different ways. He must have *stepped up to the plate*, to use a popular sporting metaphor of today: the theatre was a highly competitive place for all involved, and Will and Co. were a crack team, at the top of their game. I think perhaps Will was one of those lucky people who have natural authority, whether innate or learnt. Again, it may go back to the early, formative years with his family's disgrace: perhaps Will learnt to use his judgment, to watch what he said and to be accommodating when necessary, rather than brash and stubborn, like Ben. As previously argued, he has learnt to avoid trouble and conflict.

F. Impulsiveness/Liveliness: Score 7

Another tricky one, linked with the last characteristic. On a scale which goes from serious and prudent, taciturn even, to enthusiastic, impulsive and heedless, once again, you come up against the enigma that is Will Shakespeare and the dichotomy of his personality. Outwardly gregarious and animated, he is not as happy-go-lucky as he appears to others. He has a serious side, obvs. Look at his output. Though this was a time when playmakers were regarded, at least to start with, more as jobbing craftsmen than serious writers, this was to change, and Will played a major part in the revolution. His plays body forth the sheer passion he felt about what he was doing, the desire, as his career progressed, to say what *he* wanted to say and not just to entertain audiences.

G. Conscientiousness: Score 6

A high score here would indicate someone rule-bound and moralistic, which would not seem to be a personality fit with Will. In his plays he often mocks the pompous, the prim and proper characters like Polonius and Malvolio. Those who can't see the wood for the trees, those who are *up themselves,* as we'd say today.

Will can act with boldness when under pressure, as, for example, in making the biggest decision of his life and heading for London.

On the other hand, I get the feeling that Will needs some discipline in his life and responds well to it: he feels obligations and doesn't ignore rules. He has a sense of duty to family and conforms outwardly when necessary – i.e. most of the time in Elizabethan England. Perhaps in this way he is more circumspect than his father.

H. Venturesomeness/Social Boldness: Score 8/9

Will's chosen career and whole existence suggest a high score here: he isn't shy or timid and has always been able to talk to people from all walks of life, which has proved invaluable. He has a spontaneity about him but will have to rein it in sometimes, for example at court, where a fulsome, subservient manner is required. He is an actor, after all! His double life informs his behaviour in so many situations.

I. Sensitivity: Score 5

The terminology here can be a bit misleading: at the top of this scale would be someone who is so hyper-sensitive, so turned in on himself or herself as to lose all objectivity and awareness of others. This is not Will. Yes, he is deeply intuitive and sensitive, evidenced by his writing. He has that rare ability to communicate on an instinctive emotional level with us today, four hundred years after his death, as well as with his original audiences. However, in life, he was self-reliant but not self-absorbed.

L. Vigilance/ Suspiciousness: Score 6/7

Another tricky one in which you have to weigh up the persona of the *gentle* character, often described by contemporaries, but also take into account the survival tactics required to flourish in the world Will inhabited. Will was probably not as trusting as his affable exterior would have suggested to those who knew him as an acquaintance. Underneath he must have been alert to danger. He probably didn't need the cunning of the politician or courtier – though his plays show time and time again that he understood it – but he may well have been secretive at times, devious in his double life.

M. Imagination: Score 7

You'd think Will would get top marks here, but again we're talking personality constructs, rather than analysing his plays. Though Will, the writer, was highly imaginative, almost off the scale, when you consider his stories, his use of imagery, his dreamscape settings, he must have been surprisingly practical. He was certainly not absent-minded about money and business-matters, for example. There is enough of a paper-trail to show that he was financially shrewd and also litigious, involved in various court cases, seeking redress for wrongs or payment of debts, for example. He must have enjoyed doing business deals, especially buying property and land.

Yes, I'm sure he was lost in fantastical worlds of the imagination at times, but he knew the external realities of life and paid attention to them.

N. Privateness/Shrewdness: Score 7

This really follows on from the last section. I would like to think there was a guileless, open side to Will, but I wonder if it was a bit of an act. Again, he's a mixture; he is astute, diplomatic, even calculating, when occasion demands. You only have to read his plays to understand how socially aware he is. He has a worldly side which has definitely helped him to cope in the dog-eat-dog world of 16/17th century London. And he is probably keeping part of himself very private.

O. Guilt-Proneness: Score 4

Will is self-assured and confident – he is not afraid to seize the day. Were he at the top of the scale here, he would be very, very troubled, a constant worrier, almost paranoid with anxiety over some things. However, he clearly has a strong self-belief, trusting in his artistic talent, always knowing, deep-down, that he is as good as, if not better than, the competition. It's likely that he inspires confidence in others, too. Throughout his life people may have thought he was older than his actual age. Perhaps Anne did when she first met him...

However, if you read his plays, you discover how well he understands the guilt-troubled soul. It's a reasonable supposition that his own anxiety and guilt, when he suffers from them, are not work-related but always to do with family.

Q1 Openness to Change: Score 9

This is an easier one, in my opinion. Will took a huge step into the unknown and went to London, after all. He doesn't fear change and can adapt to it. He is to be seen breaking the mould, both in his life and artistically, in his plays, where he doesn't follow the herd but often experiments with new formats and themes. Will has always been able to think out of the box and challenge the status quo, as do many of his characters. Liberal rather than conservative, he is, nevertheless, aware of the pull of tradition and conformity in others.

Q2 Self-Sufficiency: Score 7

Will's personality polarity is clear in this construct, as in others, and is becoming a pattern. Will is resourceful and self-sufficient. How else would he have done what he did? At the height of his creativity he doesn't need other people. He is an independent thinker and thrives on the loneliness of the long-distance writer, which is the concomitant to the gregarious side of his nature.

On the other hand, he is people-dependent in his milieu: he needs the response of the audience and he thrives on being in touch with his environment, the city of London. He feels secure in a group and interacts happily with those around him.

Q3 Resilience: Score 8

This is linked with many of the above characteristics, for example G and Q1. Will is resilient and can take the flak. Writing as a job, is highly subjective, depending on the opinions of others for success, so he has to be thick-skinned at times. The score in this personality quotient is also about degrees of compulsiveness, about precision and control. Will isn't careless and undisciplined, like some creative artists; he has an exacting, side to him, perhaps innate, perhaps instilled by Stratford Grammar School. Though used to thinking on his feet, I would imagine that he might find it difficult to sit and write in chaos: there are times when he has to get things right for his own peace of mind. But he's brilliant, for example, at completing the task in front of him – to a very tight deadline! Luckily for him his phenomenal talent for words enables him to work much of the time in broad sweeps of the brush rather than with the miniaturist's tiny precise painting-on-ivory technique. He would never have produced his amazing output of plays and poetry without this facility.

Q4 Tension: Score 7/8

This is about high tension and being *driven* – at the top end of the scale – as opposed to low tension and torpidity at the bottom. Most biographers pay tribute to the convivial side of the merry bard relaxing and letting off steam in the alehouse, but behind this endearing image, Will has high energy. He works well under pressure, often being very hard on himself if he doesn't meet his own high standards. Even through emotional turmoil and grief he uses work as an antidote and distraction. *Time's winged chariot* is always *hurrying near* and he is acutely aware of his own mortality, *the skull beneath the skin*, as are very many Elizabethans and Jacobeans.

In conclusion

No-one will agree with the scores I've given Will – readers, Shakespeare scholars, psychologists, teachers, students... It's a subjective exercise, after all, though I've tried to use some evidence from the life and works to support my analysis. I hope I've made a few plausible points and given you something to think about, even if you disagree strongly.

To refer back to my *Prologue* for a minute, I think, surprisingly, most of my analysis supports the supposition I made there, that Will Shakespeare was a bit of an enigma, a dark horse, a mystery man, etc. I've come on my own journey since writing that, trying to synthesize my thoughts with my research to produce a coherent whole. I knew the certainties of journey's end in terms of the Bard's death, the publication of the *First Folio*, and so on, but didn't know whether I'd be any closer to the real human being. I feel that I am. This hypothetical personality test may have started out as a bit of fun, but it has become something more serious.

My conclusions underline the balance and polarisation of Will's personality, and have helped me to understand more about what made him tick and how he achieved what he did.

He is warm-hearted and out-going, but secretive at times. He enjoys the company of others but doesn't always seek it out, happy to be alone at times. He thrives on interaction with people, but is self-reliant. He conforms outwardly but breaks the mould in many ways. He is self-controlled and risk-averse, but can be bold when he needs to be. He is shrewd and business-like, but his imagination flies high above the earth. He is positive, confident, at home in his environment, but plumbs the depths of despair in his writing. *Full fathom five.*

I won't go on. A trained psychologist would take the results of this test through several more stages to build a personality profile and ascertain suitability for a job, a career or training course.

I haven't the expertise, or the need. *O reason not the need!* Will would have said. In any case, Will found the perfect job for himself, a job which had not existed until he created it and wrote his own job description. He was an actor, but possibly an even better actor on the stage of his own life. He was a theatre manager and even more adept at managing the two halves of his double life, only revealing as much of himself as he wanted people to see.

Last but not least, he was a writer.

If he had learnt to control his emotions, he allowed them complete freedom to feed into everything he wrote. His acute sensitivity to the extremes of happiness and suffering in the world were a key part of his inspiration to write and to try and make sense of the human condition. The theatre gave him a wonderful opportunity to speak to an audience through his characters. And as his life went on, he became more certain of what he wanted to say to others, if they were still listening. They were. And they still are.

Finally, if there is something *on which his soul sits on brood*, it has been a driving force throughout his life, but probably no-one knows what it is, even those close to him. Perhaps he, himself, doesn't know. Though he probably does, if it has to do with his desire to make good and to recover from the bad name his family gained. It *determines* him and he is *determined: Will* by name, *will* by nature.

In conclusion, he is a rare breed, both a pragmatist *and* a man of soaring imagination, grounded, but in the clouds. In the words Arthur Miller, the American playwright, describing someone he knew with a similarly unusual personality mix, Will is *a tough dreamer*.

King James VI of Scotland, who became King James I of England.

ACT FIVE:

The Jacobean Playwright
1603-1616

1. Enter King James VI of Scotland

On February 24th 1603, the Queen died. Elizabeth was sixty-nine and Shakespeare's company had played before her at court for the last time on 2nd February, just three weeks before. *Good Queen Bess dies* might have been a headline, had there been any newspapers, or *Queen's life draws peacefully to a close* – or more cruelly, *Queen dies at last*, as she'd been ailing for a long time and characteristically refused to take it lying down, literally, only taking to her bed when too ill to stand.

After keeping everyone guessing for half a century about the fraught question of her successor, she finally gave in just before her death and named King James VI of Scotland. No surprise there, really. After all the kerfuffle, debates, attempted coups, claims and counter-claims, the son of Mary Queen of Scots had by far the best provenance to become the next monarch. The famous Elizabethan era came to a close and the next age was Jacobean, after *Jacobus*, the Latin for *James*. (Latin still rules, but the English language is thriving, thanks to all the poets and playwrights.)

In spite of the fact that the late Queen had imprisoned and executed his mother, James was well disposed to the offer of the English crown, and the English people, in their turn, were well-disposed towards him. With alacrity he accepted the invitation to rule England as well as Scotland and prepared to ride south. He had never seen his mother after the age of two, as she'd been forced to abdicate and leave Scotland; he certainly wasn't a symbol of the Catholic cause, as she had been, having been brought up with strict Scottish Protestant values. Any fears that he might want to reinstate the old religion were quickly dispelled. He was clearly a moderate and an appeaser, preferring to make friends with his enemies and entertain them at court. Elizabeth hadn't actively sought war and conquest either, but she had inherited enmity from Catholics in England and Europe as a legacy from her father, Henry VIII. By the time James came to the throne, most of Britain was peacefully Protestant and Catholicism much less of a threat – or so it seemed!

Considering everything it represented, James' accession went incredibly smoothly: probably everyone, courtiers and commoners alike, heaved a collective sigh of relief. Well, perhaps it wasn't totally smooth, as another severe outbreak of plague affected London in 1603. Shakespeare and Co. moved out to healthier areas, the playhouses were once again closed and James's coronation had to be delayed till 1604 when it was safe for him to enter London.

By all accounts, James was a bit of an oddity, a strange paradox of a man who was something of a scholar but seemed to relish the creation of a rather drunken and debauched court with none of the formality of Elizabeth's. Dour, he was not! More of a wise fool. He is supposed to have had some rather unappealing personal habits, like slobbering and picking his nose. But he spent a fortune on clothes, as Elizabeth had, so he must have been aware of his appearance and the need to look and act the king. He also fondled favourite young men, so was probably gay or bisexual, but he was married with a large family, so had done his duty for the future of the monarchy.

Both he and Queen Anne loved the theatre and were even more generous towards actors and entertainers than Elizabeth had been; he very quickly renamed Will's company *The King's Men*, giving them a unique position, legally ratified, as the foremost company contracted to play before him. He also made them *Grooms of the King's Bedchamber*, an honorary title (they didn't have to valet his clothes or anything) which meant they had an official position as court servants. This royal patronage bestowed status and respectability, not only on Will and Co. but also, indirectly, on the whole acting profession, who for some time had been going up in the world with the growth of the London theatre.

The intellectual side of James loved reading and debating, as well as writing pamphlets and books on subjects which engaged his interest, like promoting the unity between England and Scotland, creating one Great Britain and forging a British identity. He also oversaw the most beautifully worded English translation of the Bible that has ever existed, known as the King James Bible and used for centuries in the Anglican Church. A whole committee of learned scholars were commissioned by James to work on this magnum opus. There's a strange mystery about one of the psalms which has caused researchers to wonder whether Will, himself, had a hand in the translation. Psalm 46 has the word *shake* as the 46th word from the beginning, and the word *spear* as the 46th word from the end. Did Will, who was forty-six at the time, help with the wording of this psalm, encoding his own name and age as a secret joke?

2. *In my mind's eye*: London, 1604

In The Mitre, near his lodgings in Silver Street, Will sits and stares into space. This is his favourite ordinary where he can get a good meal at whatever time of day or night; Dick and Peggy, who run it so efficiently, always let their regular customers use this little back room for privacy, away from the roistering drinkers. Will has penned many a scene in here and some of his best ideas have come to him when he's dined on a goodly plate of mutton stew and a glass of fine Rhenish.

He's just been fitted for his new doublet and hose, made from a bolt of sumptuous red cloth – he knows good wool when he sees it – a gift from the new king. Odd how that sounds, to say 'king', when, all his life so far, there's been a queen on the throne. But then everything has changed. His life, his art... Still, the jacket looks well, with its intricate buttoning and fine lawn collar.

All of The King's Men – as they are now called – have been given five yards of the fabric for new livery to wear at the coronation of James VI of Scotland, now James I of England. They're royal servants, members of the court! Will smiles to himself. The lad from rural England has come far; he's Mr William Shakespeare of New Place, Stratford-upon-Avon, Gentleman, and now a Groom of the King's Bedchamber, to boot. He has an urge to tell his father how he has restored the family fortunes – why is it still about his father? But John lies beneath the sod in Holy Trinity churchyard.

The plague has finally abated and at last the dreadful bells, sounding a death knell for yet another funeral, have ceased. Will has just returned to the city. James, too, has finally been able to take possession of his kingdom, after waiting outside London, like a groom impatient for his bride.

Will runs his fingers through his thinning hair; forty years old and bald on top! Hey, ho, we shall ne'er be younger! He's written 27 complete plays now and he still feels the joy in his heart when he hears words from his own pen ring out to the multitudes in The Globe. He still feels the blood coursing through his veins before he steps onto that stage. Admittedly, the parts he plays now are usually ones with some gravitas, like the ghost of Hamlet's father, released from Purgatory (which you're not supposed to believe in now!) to walk the night, and command his son to revenge. He can sense the audience's fear, the held breath, when he climbs through the trapdoor, in full armour, his visor up, his face a ghostly white with the lead paint.

'I am thy father's spirit,

Doomed for a certain term to walk the night...'

How quickly the river of life runs on, he thinks to himself. Perhaps he should have written a valedictory poem for the Queen, but the moment has passed. Leave that for some of the other pen pushers. A strange contrast, this new monarch, this son of the dangerous Queen of Scots who threatened the English throne for so long. How far in the past that seems now. But it is said that her cousin, Elizabeth, despite her sometime ruthlessness, suffered nightmares for years about signing Mary's death warrant. Guilt. Will knows about that. Did she long for absolution, the Catholic state of grace? As he does sometimes.

But James... less grand, more familiar. Too familiar with some people, as if he doesn't know how to act the king! But at least he has a wife and children, so no anxious years of speculation about marriages and heirs which has dogged the last four monarchs... And making peace with Spain – diplomatic rather than bellicose! That shows wisdom.

Everything feels peaceful, strangely calm. Will shudders at the thought of the Essex fiasco, remembering the taste of his own fear. He thinks of the lines he wrote in his Roman play, Julius Caesar: 'Cowards die many times before their deaths/The valiant never taste of death but once.' He should have had better judgment. Is he losing his wits like poor Lear? He knows he's not, but sometimes he feels storm-tossed, dreading the wrack of his body, the softening of his brain...

Perhaps he'll write something to please James, something Scotch. The new king pretends to prefer everything from his native land, but Will knows it's a bit of play-acting; James likes the English court, likes the gentler religion, loves the theatre ... He is keen to forge a union between England and Scotland, to heal the old cicatrice, to create a Great Britain which will be stronger.

Will is reading a book he found recently at Richard Field's about Scottish history, unlawful seizure of the throne, bloodlust... In his mind's eye he sees three dreadful hags who lead a good man to his doom – the King is afeard of witches, as are most honest citizens. Will gazes into the fire: the flames have died down leaving molten core. He pictures a tale of ancient hubris, murder and mayhem, the restoration of rightness, Scotland's salvation.

3. Willpower

So, how did regime change affect Will? Whether or not he actually walked in procession at the King's coronation is not known for certain, but the gift of cloth for livery is fact. I'm sure he would have enjoyed the new recognition given to his company, not to mention the higher status of the acting profession generally; the sonnets, those personal poems, reveal some sensitivity to class and position in society, so he must have felt proud of what he'd achieved, like his father before him. Round about this time he may have commissioned the painting of a self-portrait, which would have been considerably more expensive and time-consuming than taking a *selfie* on a phone today, though King James might have obliged and put his arm round Will's shoulders! In the days before photography, people paid to have their portrait done as an outward symbol of status. One of the few authenticated portraits of Will is the stylized engraving printed in the Folio editions of his works and reproduced countless times since. This was probably taken from an earlier painting, now lost, and shows Will in a well-cut jacket, perhaps the one made from the red wool fabric given to him by James I. It would be lovely to know for sure that other paintings, thought to be of Will, were authentic. One of them, known as the Chandos portrait, shows a younger, handsomer man, instead of the older, balder guy most of us think of when we picture Will.

In 1604 Will was 40 years old, two years older than the king, and at the height of his fame, not to mention his creative powers. Even today 40 is something of a meridian point in life – was it a significant age for Will or was his son's death always the dividing point, the *before and after* by which everything was measured? By 40, Will would have been working for roughly eighteen years in the theatre; he had written about twenty-seven plays, probably collaborated on a few others, and acted in a good many more.

In 1605 the theatres had reopened, it was show-time again and *The Globe* was once again in business.

As usual life became pretty manic, what with performances there *and* at court where revivals of Will's comedies were popular with the king and queen. (The *King's Men* were to perform 187 times before James I.) And, as usual, there was a constant demand for new plays. The term *over-achiever* springs to mind when you think of what Will had already done and what he was *still* doing on a daily basis. Perhaps he stopped acting around this time, because his name doesn't appear any more in the cast lists for performances, the last bill carrying his name as an actor being for a play by Ben Jonson, *Sejanus*, which was a complete flop!

What with Will, Ben and other good playwrights out there, you could watch a glorious mix of different plays in the years following the succession of James I, the first Stuart king. The theatre was flourishing and, meanwhile, Will was ready to try something new again. *Twelfth Night*, completed between 1601 and 1602, marks the end of Will's prolific phase of writing lighter comedies; there was a more satirical, topical kind of comedy in vogue – a tad different from Will's romantic plays with their happy endings. In addition, the *Masque*, a sort of drama-and-music combo, had become popular, too. It had much more elaborate scenery and costumes, whereas the outdoor playhouses still had a fairly bare stage, minimal props, and costumes which were often the cast-offs of the nobility. Written mainly for indoor court performance, masques gave the courtiers, themselves, a chance to take part in some amateur dramatics; even the women were allowed act and sing in them, probably because these mini-dramas had an overt moral tone which made it OK for the fairer sex to participate.

Will had always kept an eye on what was in fashion, but clearly masques didn't do it for him because he never wrote one! Though he did include a few mini-masques in his plays. He'd always had the confidence to follow his instinct for what would work on stage, not always conforming, but marching out of step to the beat of his own drum. In the first decade of the 17th century that drum was playing with a sombre, riveting sound which sent shock waves through the air and shivers down the spine.

4. Why Tragedy?

When I picture the early part of the 17th century, it's coloured in dark shades of black and purple, whereas the Elizabethan era is all light blue and gold, in spite of its cruelties. Later in the 17th century there was bloodshed, civil war and revolution, when the people executed their King, Charles I, but I think my colour-coding really reflects Will's tragic sensibilities and the mega-powerful plays he produced during this time. He left the genre of romantic comedy behind him and turned to the plays for which he is arguably most famous and which are most often performed. The chronological order of Will's tragedies is thought to be: *Hamlet*, (probably written before Queen Elizabeth's death), then *Othello, King Lear and Macbeth*, all written in incredibly swift succession between 1599 and 1606. The two Roman tragedies, *Julius Caesar* and *Antony and Cleopatra*, are thought to have been written in 1599 and 1607, respectively, at each end of this astonishing period of creativity, when mood of his plays changed and Will chose to concentrate on the genre of plays he had explored least so far in his career.

The Greek Geeks

We've got the Greeks to thank for tragedy! They passed down an art form much imitated by writers of different cultures and languages throughout the centuries. Perhaps the great age of tragedy has passed now, or maybe it has widened and changed to accommodate newer literary genres, like the novel, or different media, like film. The Elizabethan and Jacobean playwrights continued the Greek tradition, retaining many of the key classical elements, like the downfall and ultimate death of the central character for whom you feel pity and fear, because there is an inevitability about what is happening and you know it won't end well. The hero is sympathetic and possesses good qualities, but contributes to his own tragedy, through a mistake or error of judgment. He is doomed, therefore, through a tragic flaw in his character, known as *hamartia*, pride or ambition being common examples.

The audience, in the collective experience of watching the play, understand the terrible trajectory of the hero's fall from grace, and the effect on the world around him, but, of course, are unable to do anything about it. The phrase *dramatic irony* is often used to describe this situation of the audience's being one step ahead of the central character, able to read the writing on the wall, but powerless to warn him.

The Greeks also believed, however, that something good came out of tragedy and that it had a cleansing power – a kind of emotional detox, called *catharsis,* for the audience who went through all the suffering with the hero; the only difference was, and still is, that *they* can walk away at the end, thinking *there but for the grace of God...* This, then, is the meaning of tragedy, as art: like lots of words, *tragedy* has been devalued and trivialised, often used very loosely now to describe anything sad or annoying, for example losing your I-phone or having your car towed away.

The Elizabethan playwrights, led by Kit Marlowe, who had huge successes with tragedies like *Tamburlaine* and *Dr Faustus*, brought new and different elements to their tragedies, while keeping the essential plot and the five-act division. They ramped up the horror, by showing more violence on stage than the Greeks had allowed. This proved enormously popular with their audiences, just as it is in films today, and continued to be included in plays of the Jacobean era. Will shows numerous fights on stage, from formal fencing bouts to battle scenes: murders, enacted or reported, range from stabbings and sword thrusts to suffocation and strangulation. Torture and punishment take place, often on stage, the most excruciating scene being that of Gloucester's blinding in *King Lear.* Suicides vary from ancient Romans honourably running on their swords, to Cleopatra's clasping a poisonous snake to her breast.

Will had already written the *Titus Andronicus, Romeo and Juliet, Richard II,* dramatizing the murder of a king who made fatal errors early in his reign, and *Julius Caesar,* showing an even more famous assassination, but when he came to write *Hamlet,* he created a new and different kind of tragedy, which broke all previous moulds.

Hamlet

For *Hamlet*, arguably the most discussed play ever, Will takes an old play and breathes new life into it, at the same time pushing out the boundaries of tragedy further than they've been stretched before. The story of a son, a prince and heir to a throne of Denmark, avenging the death of his murdered father, led to a whole spate of revenge plays being written by the Jacobean playmakers, but none was quite like Will's.

Will looks at the mental stuff going on in his characters' heads in a way which was cutting edge for the time and still feels modern today, even though the study of psychology has been invented and we're used to the bare-all and share-all methods of behavioural therapy. In his long soliloquies, solo speeches in which he opens his heart to the audience, Hamlet tells the audience what he's going through after the death of his father and the very swift remarriage of his mother to Claudius, his uncle, an incestuous union in his view. Never before had the audience been so close to the tragic hero, inside his head and privy to what he was thinking and feeling at key stages of the drama. Incredible when you know that Will's understanding of psychology came centuries before Sigmund Freud and the birth of a science which studied the subconscious mind. When Hamlet learns that his father was actually murdered by Claudius, he longs for revenge – and the blue touch-paper of the tragedy is lit.

As he wrote more plays and took his art in new directions, Will had become closer and closer to his central characters, showing them develop and *grow* as people within the bounds of the play, but in his tragedies he shifts up into top gear: the action is *driven* by the central characters and Will seems to feel their suffering in the *pith and marrow* of his own being. Hamlet is frustrated time and time again by his own nature, as well as circumstances, in his desire for revenge; more and more characters are caught up in the process which ultimately results in multiple deaths and the total annihilation of a royal dynasty.

Othello

The story of *Othello* is an altogether simpler tale, in many ways, though again so psychologically plausible, that it reaches parts that other tragedies don't reach. Again the plot follows the inevitable and painful downfall of a fallible human being, true to the classical criteria of tragedy; the Aristotelian requirement for the high status of the tragic hero is fulfilled in that Othello is an important general, though not royalty. This tale of jealousy, a more domestic and universal failing, is so tightly plotted so that you feel trapped in its claustrophobic events from the start, drawn into the suffering of the characters and the awful simplicity of the momentum towards death. The plot and themes are given additional and heightened nuances by the background and Will's fascination with other races, cultures and creeds: Othello is black, a Moor (Muslim African) and married to a white Venetian woman who fell in love with him and disregarded her father's opposition, together with all the prejudice of the time, to become his wife. Iago, another *smiling villain*, like Claudius, is eaten up with jealousy of Othello's successes, both in winning the beautiful Desdemona for his bride, and in his military career which sees him promoted to become the General in charge of the island of Cyprus.

In real life, Will was probably reading a book about Africa for information and inspiration, and he may well have met the Moroccan ambassador who, according to historians, visited Elizabeth's court. Even today when we can fly anywhere or communicate online with anyone across the world, we are still intrigued by the *otherness* of far-away lands and peoples; imagine the fascination for Will and his contemporaries, meeting foreigners, especially those of different colours and creeds, hearing travellers' tales and reading accounts by the explorers who had sailed across oceans to discover new lands. As with Hamlet, Will can get into the mind-set of Othello, imagining his thoughts and feelings, portraying his terrible vulnerability. As with Shylock, Will understands this character from another race and place, showing sensitivity to the outsider, the stranger, the incomer, when it's more than likely that he, himself, never left the shores of England.

King Lear

This play, however, *is* set on his native shores, in the feudal castles and across the blasted heaths of Ancient Celtic Britain, to be precise. It's one of the few plays that Will doesn't set somewhere abroad. The eponymous hero, King Lear, who is ruler of this ancient land, makes his fatal mistake right at the beginning of the play. It sticks out like a sore thumb – you can't miss it. Talk about the elephant in the room! Lear is an appallingly bad judge of character, and, when it comes to dividing up his kingdom, he is deceived by the flattery and false declarations of love from two of his daughters. Without thought, he hands over lands and power to them, cutting the third, Cordelia, out of her share, even though her feelings for him are genuine. She cannot *heave her heart into her mouth* and is not mercenary like her sisters. Lear goes through terrible suffering, including madness, before, like Othello, he sees the error of his ways. It's the steepest and most painful of learning curves. As the 19th century novelist, George Eliot, said: *the greatest pain comes from consciousness of error.*

Macbeth

Madness clearly fascinated Will and became a theme in several plays. Ophelia went out of her mind after her father's death and Hamlet's rejection. Hamlet, himself, feigns madness, as does Edgar in *King Lear.* Hamlet, in the pretence, comes very close to the edge of insanity, before he manages to step back from the brink. Or does he? One of the most famous mad scenes ever written is the one where Lady Macbeth is shown, riven with guilt, desperately washing her hands again and again, imagining them stained with blood – *Out, out, damned spot* – after she has aided and abetted her husband in the murder of the king of Scotland in order to seize the throne. Initially possessing great toughness of mind, Lady Macbeth loses it completely (in both senses) and leaves her husband to face the music alone and to become tyrannical, abusing his power. Eventually he meets his doom at the hands of Banquo, the force for good, from whom King James believed he was descended. Will had written his Scottish play.

Will's tragic mood

Good and evil are powerful forces, though not in an obviously Christian sense, in all of Will's tragedies. Whether you believe in the reality of the three weird sisters, the witch-like characters who lead Macbeth to his doom with their ambiguous prophecies, or regard them as the personification of evil, this play has a strong element of the supernatural, of forces controlling the lives of humans and shaping their tragic outcomes. King James, along with most people at the time, was in mortal fear of witches and persecuted many allegedly guilty of witchcraft, as well as writing a book on the subject. Even today *Macbeth* is often called *The Scottish play*, by superstitious actors who believe it is cursed and prefer not to name it in case it brings them bad luck.

What made Will turn to tragedy in these transitional years when a queen died and a new king came to the throne? Was he becoming an older, wiser but sadder person, acquainted with grief, as he was? As usual, you have to go in for some intuitive guesswork, but it must have been a conscious decision for Will, in his maturity and with fuller experience of life, to write in this genre. The great tragedies all belong together and are part of a time when Will consciously went over to the dark side for themes and characters; there's no escape here from all the defects, frailties and vices of humanity, from characters who show jealousy, hatred, naked ambition, not to mention bad judgment, greed and awesome stupidity. Will explores the inevitable consequences and dramatizes them uncompromisingly. He takes no prisoners.

This is the way the world ends/

Not with a bang but a whimper...

...according to the 20th century poet, T.S. Eliot, but Will's tragic world does end with a bang! A crash that sends shock waves through his audience. Even today, when we're attuned to grim realism in books, films and TV, we feel stunned by the endings of Will's tragedies. For many years after Will's death, the original text of *King Lear* was never performed as it was thought too dreadful and harrowing. Usually a version with a happy ending was played instead – which rather defeats the object of tragedy.

Biographers have wondered whether Will, himself, was going through a serious emotional trauma at the time he was writing the tragedies, clinical depression, a nervous breakdown, a mid-life crisis, call it what you will. He seems to understand mental fragility so well, the vulnerability of the mind to suffering, the way rationality can be lost in a split-second. Despair, distortion, disintegration: all can follow on with horrifying speed, and, again, the psychological insight is way ahead of its time.

We don't know whether Will's mind buckled and nearly broke under some kind of strain at this point in his life, whether he felt a loss of control – or even out of control. Was he wandering, like the characters in *King Lear*, in a moral and spiritual wilderness of his own? Was Gloucester's deep pessimism shared by Will at this time?

As flies to wanton boys, are we to the gods,

They kill us for their sport.

Growing to manhood, Will has been through unhappy family episodes, financial crises and his own enforced marriage. Religious faith may have brought danger close to the family – they may have lived in fear of the knock at the door from the Queen's spies. Then there have been the deaths of family members, including Will's own 11-year-old son, Hamnet. Perhaps Will has lived for years with more pressure than many could cope with: perhaps it's taken its toll. As well as the pace of work, he's led a double life, lived in two very different worlds: the bohemian world of the theatre which, through its astonishing success, has brought proximity to the politics and intrigue of the Court and, in contrast, the circumscribed life of small town Stratford, with its family commitments and more hum-drum concerns, not to mention the judgmental attitudes of its inhabitants and, quite possibly, his own relations.

Will may have been under great strain for years; he may, as experts have speculated, have also become ill with some sort of physical or mental illness, or both, at this time. In the absence of medical records, and certainly not ones like today's, there are only the plays, inadmissible evidence, to shed some light on Will's state of mind.

Were these angry years? Fearful years? Years of disenchantment with life? Was he tired of the falseness of the Court, the requirement for constant flattery and the need for vigilance all the time? Again the words he gives Hamlet, (in prose this time) can't be bettered as a description of melancholia, or depression, as it's called today:

It goes so heavily with my disposition, that this goodly frame the earth seems to me a sterile promontory; this most excellent canopy, the air, look you, this brave o'er-hanging firmament, this majestical roof fretted with golden fire: why it appeareth no other thing to me than a foul and pestilent congregation of vapours.

If Will looked wearily at the world and saw no beauty in it any more, perhaps the creative impulse preserved his sanity, channelled his emotions. Whatever his own state of mental or physical health, it seems to me that the tragedies, in their full horror, were what he wanted to write at this time, never mind the box office. Methinks it was less about pleasing the crowd and more about writing what *he* wanted: perhaps he was not in a mood to dissemble any more, to *sugar o'er* the sadness of the human predicament with more comedies or a few fancy masques!

If Will *was* religious, then I don't think there was much in the way of spiritual comfort for him at this point in his life. The argument for his agnosticism has never seemed stronger. The grim view of the gods playing cruelly with mankind, as quoted above, is the essence of tragedy and far from Christian in philosophy. There are pagan forces afoot in these plays, dominant over the frail, struggling humans whom we pity with all our hearts...

But – and there's always a *but* with Will – if there is no salvation at the end of the tragedies, then there is at least a part solution. The protagonists have achieved a kind of victory through their suffering and have learnt to see things aright – only, here's the supreme irony of tragedy – it's too late for them. Evil is punished, some balance is regained and restoration attempted after the madness, if only by those who are left behind to pick up the pieces. There is a moral rightness. As Albany says at the end of *King Lear, The weight of this sad time we must obey* – a line which has resonated with readers throughout the world in times of personal and national suffering. In the hidden copy of Shakespeare's plays, kept by Nelson Mandela and the ANC prisoners on Robben Island, it's one of many underlined sections. This, after all, is the litmus test of a great writer – one whose work has *universality*, transcending different ages, cultures, places and races of mankind.

5. Breaking News: Attempt on the King's Life 5th November 1605:

Gunpowder, Treason and Plot

James I no doubt felt triumphant about making peace with the Spanish, and bringing unity to his native country, Scotland, and his adopted country, England. Just when he must have been congratulating himself on the fact that Catholic uprisings were a thing of the past, the most serious plot of all was being hatched. The Gunpowder Plot, which the Brits still remember today with bonfires and firework displays, was designed to blow up the Parliament building when all the royal family and countless officials and nobles were present. News of it was leaked just before the whole building was blown up. James saw his escape from death as an act of God, and no doubt countless sermons were preached around the land to this effect. A man called Guy Fawkes was caught in the nick of time, just as he was to ignite countless barrels of gunpowder in the cellars of the building. Actually, he was small fry, (sorry about the awful pun) and not one of the main conspirators, though effigies of him are still burnt up and down the UK on *Bonfire Night*, as it's now called, so most schoolchildren know this story better than all the other assassination plots in their history. The chief members were hunted down and executed; many of them were from Warwickshire, that Catholic stronghold, and were almost certainly known to Will.

It was the last attempt of Catholics to gain power in England. The next period of religious strife involved the Puritans, doctrinally opposite. Even today the cellars at Westminster are ritually searched before every state Opening of Parliament.

The Tower of London today.

6. Tales, Tempests and other such Drolleries.

The writing of the tragedies probably took more out of Will than we can possibly imagine; he was 43 in 1607, and, in terms of output, slowed right down, writing only three more plays, and collaborating on a few more, as script writers today often do. I found it difficult to get my head around the random mix of things that happened to Will over the next few years, and had to draw a time-line to sort it out. I'm still not sure – nor are experts–– how much time Will spent in London during the last few years of his life: whether he ever really retired will remain a mystery. I have a mental picture of him regularly riding up and down the muddy road between Stratford and London – not exactly a rest cure.

Meanwhile, he was still a member of *The Kings Men* and still in London much of the time, closely involved with the opening of the brand new Blackfriars theatre in which he was a shareholder, as he was in *The Globe*. Soon to relinquish his position as chief writer, Will still managed to write something completely different again, a unique group of magical tragi-comedies, *The Tempest, A Winter's Tale, Cymbeline* and *Pericles*, which are often called *the late plays,* for obvious reasons, and were jokingly (spitefully?) described by Ben Jonson in the phrase at the top of this section.

Will was also engaged in doing property and land deals in Stratford, for which he would need to travel home, but there were also various other reasons for frequent journeys to Warwickshire.

There was a wedding, a christening and several funerals. In 1607 his daughter Susanna was married and her daughter, Elizabeth, Will's grandchild, was born in 1608, the same year that Mary Shakespeare, his mother, died. Will's brothers, although all younger, did not outlive him. In 1607 his youngest brother, Edmund, died in London aged 27. Edmund had followed in Will's footsteps and become an actor, but nothing is known about his career: he certainly wasn't one of *The King's Men,* though Will could doubtless have pulled strings to get him into the company. He is buried in the church which is now Southwark Cathedral and records show he was given an expensive funeral ceremony, probably paid for by Will. In 1612 Gilbert, the brother closest to Will in age, died in Stratford, and the following year his brother, Richard died. Both were unmarried with no children – unusual for those days – so it looked as if the male line of the Shakespeare family was to die out with Will, no doubt a great sadness to him.

Then there was another outbreak of plague, in 1609 which closed the theatres for over a year. It's possible that Will went home to Stratford during this time, too, and he may have written some of his last plays there. The same year Will's sonnets were finally published. *Never before imprinted* said the advertising blurb, hinting at something rather shocking within the covers – which there was, of course! I rather hope Anne never got her hands on a copy, or, if she did, that she wasn't able to read it.

Wit and Wisdom

When I described Will's last plays as *magical*, I meant it literally: the supernatural is a key theme in the group also known as *The Late Romances*. They are, as indicated, a mix of part comedy, part tragedy, but are very different in mood from the bleakness of the great tragedies; if Will experienced his own kind of catharsis in writing the tragedies, then somehow he *has* been purged. Working through the intensities of grief, he has steered into calmer waters again, even if his famous last play *is* called *The Tempest*. He's regained some of his natural comic bent, but somehow gone beyond, into new, part real, part fantastical worlds. Perhaps he *was* influenced a bit by the masques and their unbelievable plot lines, though Will's last plays are still realistic in that they *hold the mirror up to nature*, reflecting human behaviour in its *infinite variety*, but with a different emphasis and a fresh vision. Evil doesn't dominate, as it did in the tragedies, but nor does fun, as in many of the comedies. If the two *W*'s, *wit* and *wisdom*, have always been a trademark combination for Will, key elements in his plays which distinguish him from his contemporary writers, then these last, plays represent a unique, visionary fusion. There is still some defining wit in them, *say one part*, but an even stronger feeling of wisdom, *say two parts,* in the cocktail which represents his final work for the stage.

Wisdom is supposed to belong to the closing stages of life, of course, and Will's central characters are ageing with him – and also with Richard Burbage, the actor who played them on stage. The main character in the most famous play of the group, *The Tempest,* is called Prospero, an elderly duke who has been forced from power by his scheming brother and exiled to a fantasy island where spirits and strange creatures, good and bad, exist. Through magic, Prospero is able to prosper (sic) and reverse his fortunes: he creates a storm and shipwrecks his enemies on the island so he can show them the error of their ways – and, to provide love interest, do some match-making for his daughter on the side. What a wonderful mixture – what was Will smoking!

After suffering comes, instead of revenge, a happier ending brought about through forgiveness, repentance and reconciliation. *The Tempest,* which shows magic here as a force for good, not ill, as in *Macbeth,* has been a popular play ever since its first production and, more recently, has been given film treatment, for which it is particularly suited.

The very real hinterland to Will's dreamscape was the discovery of the *New World* and travellers' reports currently in circulation. There was also a strange but true story of explorers being shipwrecked on an island somewhere off the Bermudas, possibly told to Will at first hand. Tales of being marooned have always captured the imagination from *Robinson Crusoe* and *Treasure Island,* to *Lord of the Flies* and *The Life of Pi.*

The Tempest

Theatre goes posh

As well as making brilliant cinema today, the off-beat fantasy of *The Tempest* must have worked well in the new indoor theatre at Blackfriars in London, for which it was written. Always looking ahead, like the good businessmen they were, t*he Kings Men* had acquired this property with a view to being able to perform plays indoors in the winter when the British weather was doing its worst. With *The Globe* and *Blackfriars,* together with their court appearances, they were looking very secure indeed, covering all bases, as it were.

Many of Will's more recent plays were written for and performed at the new indoor theatre which would be lit by candlelight, making the atmosphere more intimate and allowing for more subtlety in the performance. In addition, music was especially composed for the songs in his plays. Imagine the greater possibilities for scenes of magic or the supernatural, like the statue coming to life in *The Winter's Tale*. Night scenes, *too,* like the one where Macbeth and Lady Macbeth are plotting Duncan's murder, would be much more atmospheric. It's also likely that the actors could go in for a quieter, more natural and less declamatory style of delivering their lines, because the audience would be much smaller and closer. Probably Will adapted some of his earlier plays to suit productions at Blackfriars, too. What isn't always realised is that Will (along with other playwrights) went back to his old scripts and did some rewriting throughout his career, adapting them for all sorts of reasons-different audiences, different historical occasions and different venues. He could tinker with the wording and fine-tune at will; the script was not set in stone.

The *Blackfriars Theatre*, itself, would have looked much more like a traditional theatre today, with the raised stage and proscenium arch that was to set a style for many years. In London, for example, there are many ornate Victorian theatres designed along these lines, though many 20th century designers have gone for more informal staging with theatre-in-the round, as it's called. Purpose-built indoor theatres in Jacobean London were the logical next step, after the huge success of the Elizabethan buildings, not to mention a much more practical one, however, they inevitably made theatre-going much more of an elite entertainment, which it has remained ever since.

At *Blackfriars*, the ticket price was sixpence, as opposed to one penny or two-pence at *The Globe*, so a very lucrative enterprise for the sharers, especially as performances did not depend on the weather. However, as ordinary people couldn't afford these prices, the audience became more upmarket. The popular trend for all classes to enjoy theatre was still alive and well, but wouldn't last much longer. By the time of The Restoration of the monarchy – and of the theatres – in the 1660s, going to see a play had become an activity for a more upper class, privileged minority.

7. Swansong

Because Will's last play is thought to be *The Tempest*, many have seen it as the *swansong* of the *Swan of Avon*. Much has been made of the play's last lines where the all-controlling Prospero resigns his dukedom, forgives all wrongs and renounces his magic, breaking his light sabre – sorry, I meant *staff*. Apologies to *Star Wars*, *Harry Potter*, etc., but Will got there first! He would have loved science fiction and was clearly fascinated by magic. Prospero was, after all, a *magus*, (plural m*agi*, like the Wise Men who went to visit the Christ child), a kind of occult scientist, probably based on the famous John Dee, Elizabeth's personal astrologer. After the success of his mission, Prospero plans to retire to Milan *where every third thought shall be my grave*. It's as if Will, himself, is making a formal statement, saying farewell to his art, adieu to the theatre. It's a bit like giving a speech at your retirement party, after graciously accepting your present of a gold watch or a garden bench.

Yeah, but no, but....perhaps it wasn't quite like that, though the early biographer, Rowe, paints a happy picture of Will's last years back in Stratford which has led to the tradition of a conscious plan: *the latter part of his life was spent in ease, retirement and the conversation of friends.* Will probably slipped into spending more and more time in Stratford, from 1611 onwards, distancing himself gradually from the theatre in the artistic and business sense, rather than throwing a huge party or making an announcement from the stage at Blackfriars. People didn't really retire in Will's day anyway: there certainly weren't any pensions, so the poor had to keep working till they dropped. Those with enough money could sit back and enjoy it, though, and Will certainly came into that category now.

Will Shakespeare has left the building

So perhaps not exactly a conscious decision, though he had been purchasing land and property in Stratford which indicates that he was planning to return permanently sometime. He did no more work after 1613. He was in his late forties, but at the time, life expectancy was thirty-five, which puts this in perspective. Besides, he was probably worn out, in need of a rest. Did he long to sit by the river, watching the swans? Was he weary of writing, as some lines in his sonnets seem to suggest? Or had the Muse of poetry, the creative impulse finally deserted him? Returning to Stratford to live the life of a country gentleman with his family around him, making amends for all the years spent apart, was probably beginning to look like a very attractive option, though I wonder if Will ever adapted totally to what we'd today call a significant lifestyle change.

Gone to Blazes!

There is now more proof that Will collaborated with other writers on several plays after completing *The Tempest*, so Prospero's speech wasn't the last he wrote. One of these, the play now called *Henry VIII*, was being performed at *The Globe* for the first time in 1613 when there was an accident with a canon being fired (no Health and Safety regulations in those days), and the whole building went up in flames. The great *Globe*, that iconic building, symbol of Will's success and his company's achievement, burnt to the ground, with props, costumes and play-scripts. Who knows whether some of Will's work was destroyed? There is at least one missing play that the experts know about – and there may be more. This fire could have been the deciding factor – Will was probably devastated, lacking the energy to deal with the disaster and seeing it as a sign, like the omens of Greek tragedy, indicating that he should return home to Stratford.

I'm being a bit fanciful here but we know that Will retired from London and active involvement in the world of theatre around 1612/13, leaving the business of writing plays to Ben Jonson, Thomas Middleton, Beaumont and Fletcher (a professional duo) et al. *The Globe was* rebuilt, eventually, (with a tiled roof), but Will left that to others to organise. Methinks he knew that *The King's Men* could manage without him now and that his own creative force was spent. That he had said all he wanted to say.

Will had made enough money from his multiple professions, together with his shares in the company and two highly successful theatres, to return to Stratford and live very comfortably in *New Place*. During his time in London he seems to have lived frugally, but he'd invested shrewdly in property and land – over 100 acres. These investments were all in and around Stratford, except for one slightly mysterious purchase of a house in London near the *Blackfriars Theatre*. He seems, according to the paper trail left, to have bought this house with the maximum of legal complication, involving the company in the purchase. Was it part of his double life that he was keeping from Anne? Was Will retaining a foothold in London, intending to live there sometimes (he never did), or was it some kind of business investment? A bit of all three, perhaps. Researchers into the family's Catholicism have suggested that it might have been a secret retreat, a safe house, for priests from Europe to stay in, but it seems unlikely to me. Another loose end in Will's life story which can't be completely tidied up.

Overall, though, the family links, the land and property deals, and the regular visits to Stratford over the years, are pretty good clues to suggest that he'd always regarded it as home; he was Mr William Shakespeare, Gentleman, of Stratford upon Avon. His name and the title of *gentleman* were, I think, very important to him, the outward symbol of respect, of lineage and status, of his own worth and his family's.

The only people, as far as we know, who were resident at *New Place*, were Anne and Judith, who probably lived very quietly, rattling around in that large house. There had been a lodger for a while – Will never missed a chance to improve his income and the growing legacy for his descendants. He'd known what financial failure felt like and I don't think he ever wanted to go back there.

Susanna had made a good marriage to a local doctor, John Hall, who was respected in the town and had some well-to-do patients, but also, it seems, cared conscientiously for all his patients, rich and poor. While on the subject of daughters, you'll find that in Will's final plays there are several strong father-daughter relationships, like that of Prospero and Miranda in *The Tempest*, and, as in the comedies, the young women are very sympathetic characters, though more innocent, like Ophelia. It is often assumed, then, that Will was close to his daughters, and tradition has it that he was especially fond of Susanna.

It seems that Susanna Shakespeare was the more highly educated of the two; in fact there is evidence that Judith couldn't write (from documents she signed with a cross), which seems an amazing situation for the daughter of the most literate man on the planet! It sounds as if Susanna was a bit of a chip off the old block – more like Will and *his* dad, John, in her strength of character and determined approach to life. For example, her name appears in a list of town dwellers refusing to take the sacrament one Easter, which suggests a refusal to conform, but also possible Catholic affiliation. The question of religion never goes away, does it? She also instigated and won a case of slander against someone who had gossiped about her, saying she'd been unfaithful to her husband.

All of this makes me feel rather sorry for Judith who was still at home, unmarried. Perhaps she always carried within her the grief of her twin's death, as well as being a reminder to her parents of the loss of their son. This is only speculation, but Susanna Shakespeare seems to have drawn better cards in the lottery of life. Judith had no better luck in her choice of husband, eventually marrying the son of a local family, who was taken to court over a paternity suit just before the wedding. He had apparently made a local girl pregnant – she died in childbirth – and was sentenced by the wonderfully named *bawdy court* to do penance in church. The Shakespeare family managed to commute this to a fine, but Judith must have suffered considerable embarrassment, not to mention unhappiness and breakdown of trust at the start of her marriage.

As usual, Anne Shakespeare remains in the shadows. What *was* she thinking and feeling? Perhaps she had spent most of her life in waiting mode. Had she given up hope that Will would ever return to live with her permanently in the big house where there was so much space now, compared with the crowded Henley Street home where she had started her married life? From the Latin epitaph on her grave, probably chosen by Susanna, it sounds as if Anne was a pious woman. Perhaps she had turned to her religion more and more for strength and consolation as the years had passed.

Will's remaining sibling, Joan, was still living in Henley Street, with her husband and three sons. Old family friends of the Shakespeare parents had passed on and Stratford had been through some hard times with fires, famines and fevers. Many of the younger generations would have no recollection of what it was like to live in a Catholic country, nor even one in transition between two religions. The Puritans were now growing in number and becoming increasingly involved in the running of the town; performances of plays from visiting actors' troupes would not be approved of now, even though the theatre was thriving in London. What a weird paradox! The distraction so enjoyed by Will as a young lad, was probably no longer a part of Stratford's entertainment. Watching the actors in the Guildhall was most likely where Will's journey had started; with people's lives it's always fascinating to see a pathway through random events and to trace that path back to its starting point.

Will definitely had an appointment with history, but only future generations would understand that.

Will was now an affluent member of local society, a landowner and someone who was known to have moved in court circles in London. The less educated locals probably only had a vague idea about how Will had made his money, knowing little about the theatre or the art of poets and playwrights. However, there were enough educated friends in and around town who *would* know, and with whom he could socialise, enjoying shared interests and conversations, which probably became nostalgic at times. Other consolations would include family and the comfort of his own home for the first time, not to mention the gentle Warwickshire countryside around.

It's sad to think that, if Will did settle into a calmer, quieter way of life, he didn't have very long to enjoy it. Try and imagine him sitting under the mulberry tree that he had planted in the garden at *New Place*, with his grand-daughter on his knee, or by the fire in his library, not searching for stories with dramatic potential, but, for once, reading purely for pleasure.

EPILOGUE

Will's death may have happened relatively suddenly and unexpectedly. A poem published years later, with the first edition of his plays, hints at this:

We wondered, Shakespeare, that thou went so soone

From the World's-stage to the Graves-Tyring-roome.

Will had written millions of words for so many characters to speak, but on April 23rd, 1616, his *own* lines ran out, the performance of his life over.

He died at New Place in Stratford, aged 52, on the day that was probably his birthday.

We are such stuff

As dreams are made on, and our little life

Is rounded with a sleep.

In spite of an enormous amount of research, the details of Will's death are sketchy, though the event and date were recorded in the parish register – in English, this time, unlike his birth, which was in written in Latin, as you know. But here's the strange thing – there is no information at all about his funeral service at Holy Trinity church where he's buried.

Presumably members of the family would have watched over Will's body, as was customary, and then have attended the service and the wake, which would have followed: there would have been his wife, Anne, and the two daughters, *their* husbands, and finally his sister, Joan, who was a widow and now the only surviving child of John and Mary Shakespeare. Will was entitled to be buried *inside* the church under the floor near the altar, always considered the best place, being closest to God and therefore the most hallowed. This was because, as a rich man, he had invested in a share of church tithes, *not* because he was a well-known writer. If you visit today, you'll be able to see the grave in the chancel; buried alongside are Anne, their daughters and husbands.

How many friends attended the funeral? How many Stratford townsfolk or councillors? How many members of local landowning families? Will was probably better known in Stratford as a local businessman: there is evidence of his dealing in corn, rent-collecting and money-lending as well as the transactions of property and land. How many from London would learn of his death in time to travel to the funeral? Probably the answer is very few: neither those from the world of the theatre, including his close friends and colleagues from *The King's Men*, nor members of the court, nor the rich patrons, for whom he had written, would have known immediately of his death, until letters came from Stratford. So if most of the mourners were local, it's still odd that no record remains of the funeral ceremony – Will was, after all, interred in a place of honour in the church and must have been one of Stratford's famous sons. But, some bits of paper miraculously survive through centuries and others don't – it's always a lottery.

Moreover, in London, there seem to have been few eulogies written about him, in spite of the fact that they were often composed for anyone famous, including actors, playwrights and theatre-managers, now acclaimed celebrities of their time. Will, as we know, had fulfilled all these roles for many years. Perhaps the explanation lies in the fact that he had faded out of the public consciousness. Though his plays certainly hadn't. The theatre was flourishing, as were *The King's Men*: they were still performing many of Will's plays, at Blackfriars in the winter and *The Globe* in the summer, but Will had retired from the scene – literally. Perhaps many theatre-goers didn't realise for some time that he had died as his plays were still out there and popular, though probably not performed as often as they had been. Add to this the fact that writers and other creative artists are often not fully valued in their own time; only with the perspective of history is their true worth and significance understood.

A very real fear

The thing that catches your eye, if you visit Will's grave in Holy Trinity Church, is the blessing, accompanied by a rather scary warning, inscribed on it:

> *Good friend, for Jesus' sake forbear,*
>
> *To dig the dust enclosed here.*
>
> *Blest be the man that spares these stones,*
>
> *And cursed be he that moves my bones.*

Was this Will's last little joke? If he wrote it, then his last bit of poetry is not his best. It sounds more like the little doggerel rhymes that the unsuccessful suitors of Portia found when they opened the wrong caskets in *The Merchant of Venice*.

But I think Will genuinely wanted his mortal remains to rest in peace, to ensure they were not disturbed, perhaps being moved to an ossuary below the church; many people at the time had a genuine fear of exhumation, of their bones being thrown into a charnel house to make way for other burials. Perhaps Will had seen too many plague pits to joke about such matters. Being flippant for a minute, perhaps he wanted to make sure that Anne wasn't buried with him.

Whatever the reason, the warning seems to have worked, though there are rumours of various attempts to desecrate the grave, together with claims that his skull was removed and taken to be buried elsewhere. Would *you* want to risk being cursed, like those who broke open the tomb of King Tut in his pyramid? However, there has recently been an investigation of the grave using sophisticated laser technology which doesn't disturb the remains in any way, an ideal way around the problem. Not only did they find that Will and the other members of the family were buried in winding sheets in shallow graves, not in a vault, as first thought, but they also found evidence of repair to Will's tomb, suggesting that the story of the skull's theft might be true.

With the discovery of DNA, there must now be a possibility that a lot more information about Will, including the reason for his death, could be learnt if his body were exhumed. However, at the time of writing, the Bard's wishes are being respected and applications refused. However, the fascination with Will's story goes on and researchers never give up the quest for new evidence… watch this space.

Was Ben there at the end?

Local hearsay was that Will caught a fever when carousing with Ben Jonson and Michael Drayton in Stratford. Drayton, a poet, lived nearby, but had Ben just popped up from London? It's perfectly possible that he might have visited his old friend and rival several times to chat over old times: he's supposed to have walked to Scotland once, so perhaps he'd called on the way to see Will, to do some serious drinking and enjoy a bi' o' banter for old times' sake.

It's also possible that Will *did* catch his death: without antibiotics, colds and fevers could turn into pneumonia and prove fatal very quickly. His sister's husband had died just before Will, which makes you suspect a possible fever epidemic of some kind in Stratford, for example typhus. Perhaps Will was in poor health anyway, worn out by the relentless pressures of his life, having over-worked for two decades. Fifty-two was higher than the average life expectancy in England at the time.

There has also been some speculation that Will had a cerebral haemorrhage of some kind, based on detection of some swelling of the temporal artery around the eye, thought to be visible in the First Folio portrait. It's a plausible idea, given the kind of life Will led, involving intense physical and mental pressure, which can often result in death for this reason. Richard Burbage, himself died of a brain haemorrhage some four years after Will. It's frustrating to think that Will's son-in-law was a doctor and that he must have treated him, but again there are no records, only those of later patients.

Last Will and Testament

Over the centuries, the thing that's caused the most controversy is Will's will! Researchers have wrestled for years with the ramifications of this document and just what inferences can be drawn from some of its stranger sections, not to mention the fact that Will changed it just before he died.

Early in the New Year of 1616, Will had the first draft drawn up. His signatures on it look rather shaky, which suggests that his health was deteriorating. Then his daughter Judith married and there was the sex scandal surrounding her new husband, Thomas Quiney, who admitted to the charge of *carnal copulation*. Will decided to revise the document, limiting the bequests to Judith and making conditions to ensure that her husband couldn't get his hands on any money. Shrewd to the end was our Will, which in itself seems to rule out a sudden death from something like a serious stroke or brain haemorrhage.

Most of his estate was left to Susannah, her husband and heirs, *plural*: though Susanna had had no more children after her daughter's birth, there was always the possibility she *might* and Will may have been hoping for a grandson. In addition, there were various other specific gifts of money left to family and friends, including some to members of *The King's Men*, with which to buy mourning rings, a common tradition.

Will had clearly reacted strongly to the disgrace of Judith's marriage, but here's the rub: there is only a brief mention of Anne and certainly no endearments like *to my beloved wife I bequeath...* Anne is left one item, the *second best bed*. This bequest is scribbled in untidily above a line of elegant script, presumably by Will's lawyer, as an afterthought. Was this all there was for Anne? It's hard to ignore the obvious conclusion that Will and his wife were not on good terms – though researchers, looking into legal practice at the time, have countered this by saying that Anne would *automatically* have inherited one third of her husband's estate, as her widow's entitlement, the right of dower. So perhaps Anne and Will had discussed everything and were in full agreement over the legacies to their children – after all she would be comfortably off for the rest of her days with her widow's share. But the bed – what was that about? Was it the marriage bed? Was it a bed Anne had brought with her from Shottery?

Granted that four-poster beds were substantial bits of furniture in those days, it still seems odd to itemise it like this, to the exclusion of all else. Carole Anne Duffy in her poem about Anne imagines that the item is included as a last message of love from Will:

Some nights I dreamed he'd written me, the bed

A page beneath his writer's hands...

In the other bed, the best, our guests dozed on,

Dribbling their prose.

Commentators, however, have found it a curious anomaly that Will's compassion for his fellow humans shines through almost everything he wrote, but the tone and nature of the bequests in his will seem to lack generosity a tad! Perhaps the experts are reading too much into it, *thinking too precisely on the event.* (Will again.) The *Immortal Bard* certainly seems to be favouring one daughter over the other and there is this very strange afterthought about the bed. Probably it's just the legal jargon which makes it sound so cold, something of an anti-climax after all the wonderful words written by Will. By necessity, wills are not emotional documents, though the legal-speak *can* be softened by words of love and gratitude. In spite of all the academic debate, the simplest answer may be that Will was close to death and the document was drawn up in some haste, never getting as far as the fair copy.

All of this must give us pause.

The last rites

So must the piece of hearsay that Will died a Papist: did he – as his father is supposed to have done – receive the last rites and sacraments of the Roman Catholic Church? In his lifetime Will seems to have avoided being caught up in the conflicting doctrinal issues which exercised so many people over the previous century, from the monarch down, and which caused on-going cruelty and violence. Yet, experts now agree that there is considerable evidence to show that the Shakespeare family clung to the old religion, that they were not good Protestants and possibly were openly defiant at times, showing their allegiance to the Church of Rome. It's also certain that distant Arden relatives were accused of being implicated in Catholic plots and that some died on the scaffold for their faith. Probably Will's Catholicism was hushed up for years, like the enforced marriage.

Will's religious allegiances remain a mystery, like so much else about him: some biographers suggest that he may have continued to practise the old religion clandestinely, as many did, but surely he would have been found out and seen as a dangerous man to be allowed entry to court. At best his plays would have been banned and at worst he would have been arrested, interrogated and his house searched, as happened to the musician, Thomas Byrd, who came from a known Catholic family. Reprisals usually followed and punishment – usually capital – if there was any hint of conspiracy to commit treason. As far as we know – which isn't very far – Will he was never questioned about his faith, though there may have been suspicions regarding the Shakespeare family. Perhaps Will was on a list somewhere, or perhaps he was known as a *safe* Catholic – not practising and certainly not *radicalised*, as we would say today – of whom there were a number at court, protected by some of the wealthy nobles or patrons. Another conundrum.

Maybe Will didn't possess the religious fervour or blind faith of some family members, whether close or distant; more interested in secular issues, he preferred to stand back from it all, watching from the wings, as it were. Maybe he lost any faith he had originally, possibly, just possibly regaining it towards the end of his life, when he was working on the last plays, which speak of forgiveness and consolation and offer a kind of redemption. Whatever his conviction, or lack of it, throughout his life, perhaps his deepest instinct, on his deathbed, was the wish to die, according to the rites of the old church, to which his family had clung in the face of the Protestant Reformation.

After Will's death, the family had a life-size head and shoulders effigy made of him, which was put in the church near to his tomb as a memento mori. If you visit Holy Trinity in Stratford today, you'll find it high up in a niche on the wall, holding a quill pen and staring into space, as if in the act of composing the next line. The bust was made in 1623 by an eminent sculptor who wouldn't have known Will, but would have either worked from a portrait, or death-mask. The family are reported as saying that it was a good likeness, History tells us that it was painted originally in life-like colours with Will wearing a scarlet doublet, but that it was later whitewashed over to make it look more 'classical'. This faux-pas was corrected and the statue was repainted later, though I have to say that the skin tones aren't the most natural and make Will look as if he's had a spray tan.

Will's family were to die out within a few generations, in spite of the large number of children born to John and Mary Shakespeare. Anne, his wife, died in 1623, aged 67, and was laid to rest alongside her husband. Susanna died in 1649 and Judith in 1662, aged 77. Susanna had no more children. Judith produced three sons but all of them predeceased her: her firstborn, christened *Shakespeare*, died in infancy and her other two boys died aged nineteen and twenty-one. Will's granddaughter, Elizabeth, married twice, into the aristocracy for the second time, but had no children with either husband. The only descendants of the Shakespeare line, still living today, are from Joan Hart, Will's sister, which seems sad after John and Will's struggle to be granted what proved a redundant coat of arms.

Sir William

There is, however, the possibility that Will had an illegitimate child. On journeys between London and Stratford, Will regularly lodged with the Davenants who ran *The Crown*, in Oxford; he was friendly with them – perhaps more than friendly with the wife and landlady, Joan, who gave birth to a son named William, to whom Will was godfather. The boy grew up to be Sir William Davenant, a poet, playwright and theatre manager who was knighted for his services to the theatre, which he helped to re-establish after the Restoration of the Monarchy in 1660. If you think this sounds like more than a coincidence, I wouldn't blame you, but Sir William may have enjoyed a little game of pretence, rather like those played by so many of Will's characters in his plays. Either he knew himself to be Will's love child – or he got a kick out of pretending he was!

There are other links, too, which add to the feasibility of the story. Sir William Davenant was the original owner of the Chandos portrait, one of the few paintings of Will which is thought to be authentic. How did he end up with this painting in his possession? In addition, Shakespeare's first biographer, Nicholas Rowe, is supposed to have sent an actor from William Davenant's company on a fact-finding mission to Stratford for him. Perhaps he knew more than he lets on in the book, but no one is sure of the date when the actor, Thomas Betterton, went to Stratford and whom he met – whether, for example, he was in time to talk to Susanna, Judith or Joan before they died, which would have made the information for Rowe's book so much more valid and valuable. As regards the paternity issue, without DNA tests, it will always be a mystery. I've discovered some online tweets from *The Ghost of Sir William* Davenant, so perhaps someone should ask him what the truth really was!

And finally... the legacy of the plays

To the memory of my beloved, the author, Mr. William Shakespeare, and what he hath left us. (Ben Jonson, Preface to the *First Folio*.)

Thank the Protestant heavens and all the Catholic saints for two members of *The King's Men* and close friends of Will, Henry Condell and John Heminge! We would never have Will's plays today, or only a few of them, if it hadn't been for their work and dedication.

As indicated, there was a strange silence after Will's death, which lasted for a few years. It's odd that for someone who had a shrewd understanding of business and legal affairs, Will seems to have been incredibly casual about protecting the works of his pen, unlike Ben Jonson, who was fastidiously careful and published all of his writing in grand folio editions for the playgoers and future generations to read. Perhaps, in this way, Ben was more *au courant*, aware of the need to preserve literature and, incidentally, of the growing popularity of *reading* plays, as well as going to stage performances. As you know, Will's narrative poems *had* been published, as had the sonnets, but of the plays only *about half* had been printed, in small, rather inferior editions, called quartos. Quality publications could have been a lucrative side-line for Will, but he doesn't seem to have been bothered, remaining more focused on his acquisitions of property and land. Did Will, in spite of all his hard work, still not see his plays as the kind of literature that would endure? Or had he simply not got around to it? Something on his bucket-list.

The two actors from the Kings Men, John Hemminge and Henry Condell, were entirely responsible for one of the most important, also, nowadays, one of the most valuable, books in the world. They must have worked tirelessly, *to keep* the *memory of so worthy a Friend and Fellow alive, as was our Shakespeare.* They clearly saw the publication of Will's plays as a final service they could undertake for their friend after his death, wishing to preserve his memory as well as the works of his pen. The two actors, who were also sharers in the company, generally played smaller parts on stage, but were to play a huge part in the history of English and world literature. Though, of course, they didn't know it at the time. Without their efforts in organising the printing of this super-sized book, many of Will's plays would almost certainly have been lost for ever.

It was a labour of love. Literally.

Love's Labours Won

As they say in the Preface to the *First Folio*, they did it *without ambition either of selfe-profit, or fame.* However much admiration and respect they had for the plays as literature, it's unlikely they'd have performed this huge task without feeling enormous affection for Will, their co-actor, director, business partner and close friend. It must have taken over their lives, involving time, energy and, almost certainly, financial cost. They would have taken a gamble on printing the complete works of Shakespeare, guesstimating how many to have printed and how many would sell. The literacy rate in England at the time was still low, about 30% of adult males could read, and it was going to be an expensive book, only affordable by the well-to-do.

Gathering together all the plays wasn't easy for a start – there must have been so many different copies floating around; even if the *King's Men* had always been meticulous about locking away scripts, there'd been that fire at *The Globe* and a lot of manuscripts could have been burnt. Available to the two actors must have been a whole mix, legally the property of the company, including handwritten *fair* copies, made by Will or a scribe, *foul* copies, i.e. his rough drafts, prompt copies and the actors' *sides,* with just their parts written out. Then there would be various corrupt or pirated versions doing the rounds. Finally, there would be the published quartos, small printed copies of Will's plays, but only about two thirds had ever reached this stage so, were it not for Hemminge and Condell, we would never have plays like *The Tempest, Macbeth* and *Antony and Cleopatra.* All in all, there must have been over twenty years of Will's work to sift through. Incidentally, the archive used by the two players has never been found. It's unlikely these papers are still lying hidden in a dusty attic somewhere, but you never know.

Memory keepers

Hemminge and Condell, though not scholars, were the best qualified people to undertake this work, knowing where everything was kept, which copies were sound and which corrupt, even which versions Will had preferred. They strove to preserve the authentic, most accurate versions of the plays for publication and, as they also state in the preface, were keen to eliminate all the dodgy copies doing the rounds, often stolen by rival acting companies. They'd worked with Will, day in day out, acted in so many performances, listened to him directing rehearsals, watched him act parts, himself. No doubt as they gathered everything together, so much of it would be so familiar: they probably heard the plays in their heads, heard Will's voice telling the company how he wanted a line spoken. As Hamlet says to the players who come to court at Elsinore:

Speak the speech, as I pronounced it to you, trippingly on the tongue: but, if you mouth it, as many of your players do, I had as lief the town-crier spoke my lines.

But there were also some permissions needed to print: the company would own most of the plays but not all. There were no such things as intellectual rights or copyrights and authors didn't earn royalties like they do today. For example, the *First Folio* didn't contain Will's late play, *Pericles,* because of legal complications, and it was only printed in later folios.

In addition, Hemminge and Condell took the trouble to organise various prefaces and eulogies to Will to be composed by notable poets, including Ben Jonson, these preliminaries being a vital part of preserving Will's memory.

Thou art a monument, without a tombe

And art alive still, while thy Booke doth live

And we have wits to read, and praise to give.

The actors also decided to include a picture of Will, not standard practice at the time and bound to incur more expense. They commissioned a copper plate etching by a young engraver, Martin Droeshout, who wouldn't have known Will and who would have had to use a painting of him as his source of reference.

It was for gentle Shakespeare cut...

Could he but have drawn his wit,

says Jonson, endorsing the good likeness of the etching...

The resulting image is the one with which everyone is familiar. It appeared in most of the folios and has been reproduced millions of times since in editions of Shakespeare's plays.

Finally, the *First Folio* was dedicated to the two brothers, the Earls of Montgomery and Pembroke, the latter being William Herbert, already mentioned as a possibility for Mr W.H. of the sonnets. No doubt this dedication would ensure their patronage and help with sales: the earls might have also contributed to the costs.

With everything good to go, the two players employed blind printer, William Jaggard, and his son, Isaac, to print the book. Years before, Will had had a disagreement with this firm of printers over their publication of some of his sonnets without permission in a collection called *The Passionate Pilgrim.* Maybe Hemminge and Condell didn't know this or perhaps they felt that

Jaggard and Son owed them one? Or perhaps it was just a case of *Better the devil you know*, which could have applied here.

Was it a good job? Well, yes and no. It was competent but there were all sorts of discrepancies arising from the use of different typesetters. However, given the laborious process of printing in those days with so many possibilities for human error, it wasn't too bad, though every version ended up slightly different. During the process – like builders who leave one job to fit in another smaller one – Jaggard and Son sometimes took on more urgent work from time to time, so the printing the *First Folio* took two whole years. By God's holy trousers, the two actors must have been tearing their hair out in frustration.

In spite of all the delays and errors, the resulting edition of the plays was pretty impressive in size and appearance, with its expensive Normandy rag paper and choice of bindings. You could even purchase the pages and have them bound in leather of your own choice, to suit taste and pocket. The resulting *First Folio,* (from the Latin for *a leaf*), published in 1623, seven years after Will's death, was a large book, roughly thirteen by nine inches, containing 36 of Will's plays, half of which had never been published before and could now be read by everyone. They were *not* in the order Will wrote them, and modern readers find it confusing, for example, that *The Tempest*, the last complete play he wrote, comes *first* in most collected editions. Hemminge and Condell, tried to divide the plays into their different genres, which was somewhat artificial, as not all the plays could be fitted easily into specific categories, a point which has already been touched on.

The choice of folio dimensions was unusual, but practical because only a book this big could accommodate all Will's plays in one volume. Folio publications were usually reserved for grand books, like Bibles, *not* plays which still didn't count as serious literature. But times they were a changing. The actors may have got the idea from Ben Jonson who'd printed an impressive folio collection of *his* plays, despite being mocked for self-aggrandisement, which was probably like water off a duck's back to him.

Not a moment too soon

The *First Folio* edition of Will's plays sold steadily until the first run of 750 sold out so that in 1632 a *Second Folio* was produced, then a third, then a fourth. After this there were no more folio editions: the world had moved on to different kinds of collected editions which were starting to pour off the presses as Will's fame became established. Most of the known editions of the *First Folio* have been bought up and are now in the *Folger Shakespeare Library* in Washington DC. Originally the book would have cost £1, which would have been expensive for those days – now an original 1623 edition is priceless.

By the time of the *Second Folio*, Hemminge and Condell, those loyal and stalwart friends, were dead, as were all of the original *King's Men*, who would have known Will in his heyday and been the living witnesses of his incredible career. Richard Burbage had died in 1619, not long after Will, or he might have been involved in the enterprise. (The tombstone of this famous actor read simply, *Exit Burbage*.) I hope Hemminge and Condell were proud of their achievements and praised by contemporaries: only history would reveal – gradually, not immediately – how true had been their instinct to honour their friend and to preserve his plays for posterity. Did they suspect that they were dealing with the works of genius, which by its very nature, only strikes mankind randomly and rarely?

I think Ben knew, bless his cotton hose. In his eulogy in praise of Will, he called him the *Soule of the Age,* and then continued with the famous prediction: *He was not of an age but for all time...*

These words have been frequently in my head during the writing of this book and, at the end, I've given the last word to Ben, imagining what else he might say about his friend Will Shakespeare.

The Shakespeare Industry

The *First Folio* ensured the preservation of Will's plays and led to countless more editions being printed throughout generations of readers, students, scholars, actors and playgoers. Since Will's death, more and more performances have been staged in different theatres across the world. With the arrival of cinema and television in the 20th century, a huge number of film versions of the plays have been made, reaching even more people. With modern satellite technology, films *and* stage productions can be beamed across continents to link audiences who are possibly quieter, but no less enthusiastic, than those who watched in the open air theatres on hot afternoons all those centuries ago.

Moreover, the *Preface* to the *First Folio*, with its contributions by Ben and co, kick-started an industry of writing *about* Will: academic research and scholarship has grown over the centuries, resulting in biography, literary criticism and books on all aspects of Will's life and times, not to mention the necessary translations, so that people of all nationalities can read the plays and their commentaries. *Hamlet* has even been translated into Klingon!

Meanwhile, Stratford has been on the tourist map since before the last owner of *New Place*, an 18th century clergyman, got so fed up with people peering in at his windows, that he had the house demolished and a new one built. He also chopped down the mulberry tree which Will is supposed to have planted. Various enterprising individuals started to fashion souvenirs from the wood and sell them to tourists, until, like relics of the true cross, no one knew which were genuine and which were fakes!

There's a curious coincidence that the first *Shakespeare Memorial Theatre* in Stratford, built in 1879, was destroyed by fire, like the original *Globe.* A new *Royal Shakespeare Theatre*, constructed in 1932, on an adjoining site by the river, and recently refurbished, draws audiences from across the world, as well as actors wanting to perform the roles created by Will. One actor back in the 18th century, who did much to increase Will's fame and bring the plays to contemporary audiences, was David Garrick, a playwright himself and manager of the famous *Drury Lane Theatre* in London. In 1769 he organised and hosted a huge pageant and entertainment in Stratford as a 200th jubilee celebration of Will's birth. You don't need a Maths degree to work out that this was, in fact, five years too late and, actually, Will's 205th birthday! Never mind, it's the thought that counts and Garrick's huge-scale fiesta helped to establish Shakespeare as England's national poet and contributed to his god-like status.

Unfortunately, some of the celebrations were literally a wash-out, due to the terrible weather. Storms and rain swelled the Avon so much that it overflowed its banks, flooding the grounds by Clopton Bridge where the Jubilee was to take place. Even the grand marquee offered no shelter from the elements and the invited VIPs in elaborate fancy dress were wading around up to their knees in muddy water! Will would no doubt have found it amusing, if he'd looked through the windows, from his plinth in the church, towards the shining river and the water-logged banks beyond.

And finally... from Shakespeare's Birthplace, where this narrative started, to the site of *New Place*, where he died, is only a short stroll in Stratford, but going via London, as Will did in life, takes a bit longer. Half a century in his case. He lived at the interface of two different worlds, just as we do today with the huge technological revolution that is taking place. There was the old, semi-mediaeval, Catholic England into which Will's parents were born, and the new Protestant land of Renaissance learning which saw Will's birth. His was an age of discovery, entrepreneurship and exploration, when a new, United Kingdom was forged and became a force to be recognised across the trade routes of the world. Acutely sensitive to the myriad convulsions of his age, he thrived on his London life at the epicentre of it all.

It was also one of those rare times of happenstance; the popular new art form, writing plays for theatre performance, came into being at the same time as Will Shakespeare, a man of prodigious talent and winning ways with words, was born. Will did far more than just contribute to the rise of the drama – he gave it impetus and power, seriousness, shape and status. Against the background of growing enthusiasm for theatre, from the monarch down to the man or woman in the dirt-strewn street, he produced an incredible pantheon of plays: he made his audiences laugh and cry and reflect on what they'd seen and heard. And go back for more.

Befriend the Bard! Now you know his story; his plays are still taught and performed in the original language which is a vital link with the long-ago world in which he lived, when so much was different but the human essentials were the same. No one has taken the English language further, in terms of expressing its versatility, adding to its vocabulary and establishing it firmly as the main language of the people, which was by no means the case at the time he was born, when educated people regarded Latin and French as superior.

Befriend the Bard! If it helps, remember that at almost every performance of a play by him, there is someone in the audience who has never seen one of his plays before. It might be you! If it helps, try not to treat him as a god or even a genius: chuck out the reverential attitude and think of the enigmatic but real person behind the word-flow. The element of mystery surrounding this man *can* be liberating, freeing you up to draw your own conclusions, just as you can take what you will from his writing which continues to resonate in different ways with each new era. I can guarantee that, if you look, you will find something in it for you, words which make your spine tingle or a thought so illuminating that you wonder at its wisdom and relevance after so much time has passed. And if you do go to a performance, you can experience the same visceral human connection he made with his first audiences all those years ago by the Thames, which is still strong today, four and a half centuries later.

Befriend the Bard!

In my mind's eye: Thoughts about Will Shakespeare by Ben Jonson

He was not of an age, but for all time. I see that clearly now. I knew it all along, really, but tried to pretend otherwise. And now he's dead and gone. Taken from us in the Spring-time, with the soft rain falling, like tears, on his little town. England's heart.

Forsooth, he did me favours, looking o'er my poor plays when no-one else was willing. Will was willing! How did I repay him? By sneering and sniping. No shame but mine. Our Will wasn't a man to bear a grudge. I was, I know, for I was envious of his gift. Beware the green-eyed monster, he'd have said.

He and I, we shared a background of grammar schools, the classics imprinted on our brains. Our paths to play-making. Yet I twitted him about his little Latin and less Greek, because I was too proud and thought I was the better scholar, taught by a renowned London master, not a rustic pedant somewhere in Middle England!

But here in the seething masses of the Globe, how we strove for glory! How we lusted after those strumpets, Fame and Fortune! We lusted after all manner of other things which I won't divulge...

By God's holy bones, I was mad-brained, when my blood was up. I hated my bricklayer step-father, an oaf, a brute, a muck-heap turd. Will, though, he loved his father – the failed alderman, so proud of his lineage and chivalrous deeds gone by. Their new coat of arms and motto, Not Without Right – 'Not Without Mustard', I quipped, trying to thrust deep with my sharp wit, cut him down to size. I saw his itch for status, just below the skin. Betimes he'd fight back with skill, words as weapons, fencing without swords, but just as often he'd smile, ignoring my blunt behaviour, as though he could see into my heart. O rare Ben, he'd call me. O rare Ben!

Then he'd dash off a Christmas comedy, in sportive humour, or make the heart leap with lines of love. The swan of Avon, gliding along, the slipstream behind him. It looked so easy, it drove me to distraction. Literally. From the Latin distraho, meaning to pull apart.

Of course it wasn't always smooth-gliding, any more than the swan's motion. He worked far into the night. And he was nearly pulled apart, driven to distraction, himself, in the dark time of his life when he lost all his mirth. I know that. Richard Burbage knew it. I don't think any other man did – no, nor woman neither. Will was inventing The Prince of Denmark and foolish Lear, when we were scribbling satire to disdain the times: he was forging Macbeth and the Moor in the furnace of his brain, when we were making masques, so my lord could stride upon a stage, pretending to act – pretenders were we all.

How did he know which bits of fustian fiction would make the best plots for plays? Which bits of a clown's motley could be turned into beautiful silken suits of pure poetry? His gift for transforming was something you couldn't put a price on – and he could put a price on most things! So can I, I have that bastard virtue, too.

I longed for his sure instinct. His ability to choose aright time after time, the best tales to make into new stories, the saddest and happiest scenes. And the noblest characters. They were real as the nose on my face! They were indeed people who walked this earth, who loved and laughed and loathed, as you and I.

And, most marvellous of all, to choose the best words. Where did his river of words flow from, his potent music? If you have read every Roman poet to inspire you, you still won't come within an English mile of him! He could create a whole speech entire in his brain, so that he scarcely blotted a line when he set it down. Would he have blotted more, I said with bile, implying imperfection, suggesting the speech needed more work. It didn't.

S'blood! I'm too clever for my own good. He was clever and good. And a rogue too. He could make the whole playhouse piss themselves with laughing, but he showed them beauty, he helped them grasp at wisdom. The cheekiest apprentice, the coarsest fishwife, the most devious courtier – he spoke to them all. He held them in the palm of his hand.

Heminge and Condell, those honest fellows, are saving the dog-eared scripts, those precious papers – to keep his memory green, to imprint every page he penned. Thank God for them! He was always careless – poor art, he'd say. The performance was all, for him.

I wish he could join us now at the Mermaid, set the table on a roar again, his eyes sparkling. Or meet us for gossip – who's in, who's out. Or for quiet conference over the mulled wine, went-the-day-well leading to any subject under the sun.

Fear no more the heat of the sun, Will, Bard of Avon.

I loved him this side of idolatry. We shall not look upon his like again.

The end

Shakespeare's Globe, Bankside, London. Founded by Sam Wanamaker,
this reconstruction of the original playhouse opened in 1997.

The Royal Shakespeare Theatre, Statford-upon-Avon,
built 1932, with major renovation in 2010.

SHAKESPEARE'S LANGUAGE

Frequently Asked Questions

1. Why is it difficult?

There are three main reasons:

- The problem with any text from past centuries is that some of the language can be obscure because it's fallen out of use. Language is constantly changing. The further back you go, the more difficult it becomes. Much of Will's language, over 400 years old, is fortunately still recognizable to English speakers today, compared with, say, that of the 14th century poet, Chaucer, called *Middle English,* which almost looks like a foreign language.

- Many of the references are obscure, too, and need explanation: they may allude to current, topical issues from contemporary life that we don't know about; they may, for example, be geographical, historical, scientific, medical, political, legal, mythological or religious references. Take the last one: though Shakespeare is not writing religious drama, he often refers to the Bible which even the uneducated and illiterate knew far better than we do today, as everyone was required by law to go to church.

- Will Shakespeare was writing, for the most part, in poetry, always a more elevated, imaginative and less literal form of language.

2. Why poetry?

Will Shakespeare, along with other playwrights in the Elizabethan and Jacobean times, was writing in the tradition of poetic drama. At the time he lived, poetry was king and still the most highly respected of the literary genres; the dramatists, led by Christopher Marlowe, were all breaking new ground in the way they adapted *blank verse* for the purposes of dialogue.

3. What sort of poetry?

Blank verse, or iambic pentameter, is unrhymed. It has ten syllables per line, which means there are five metric feet, each with one unstressed, then one stressed syllable, forming an iambus. This verse form came originally from Italy, but it happened to fit well with the natural stresses and rhythms of the English language, so writers could adapt it for dramatic purposes. *Blank verse* would quickly become second nature to Will and other writers with a good sense of rhythm. Of course, Shakespeare was an actor, too, so had the advantage of learning and speaking lines regularly, both his own and those of other dramatists.

Try reading these few lines from *Macbeth*. It isn't easy to start with, but go with the flow and see whether you can hear the rhythm:

Tomorrow, and tomorrow, and tomorrow,

Creeps in this petty pace from day to day,

To the last syllable of recorded time;

And all our yesterdays have lighted fools

The way to dusty death. Out, out, brief candle!

Life's but a walking shadow; a poor player,

That struts and frets his hour upon the stage,

And then is heard no more:

It's rhythmic but not *too* rhythmic – which would send you to sleep after a bit! Shakespeare breaks up the regular pattern of stresses from time to time, as in *Out, out, brief candle* – where you have 4 heavily accented words all coming together for emphasis.

It's always a good idea to read poetry out loud, if you possibly can. This might seem obvious in the case of a play by Shakespeare, given that it was always intended to be spoken on stage, but this important first step, vital to understanding, is often overlooked.

Most professional actors, with a bit of help, can get pretty good at speaking Shakespeare's language, even if they're more used to appearing in modern films or thrillers on TV. The actor, Adrian Lester, has said, on taking the role of Othello for the first time, 'You can't mumble, shrug and modernise your way through... you have to *feel* the iambic.'

4. Doesn't this make the plays less realistic?

Yes, in style, because people don't usually speak in verse. But nor do they sing to each **other** as in opera and musicals! We accept different art forms for what they are: there is always a certain amount of artifice involved in art, in order to develop stories and treat the big themes. Even your favourite soap has been scripted and works to a kind of formula.

5. Didn't Shakespeare sometimes write prose, too?

Yes, he did. Look through the text of a Shakespeare play and check out how much of the play is written in verse and how much in prose – the latter is easy to spot as the print goes right across the page and isn't set out in lines with a capital letter at the start of each one. You'll find that Shakespeare moves from verse to prose to verse again in all of his plays, the ratio varying in each play.

He chose to use prose for various reasons – when writing a comic scene, for example, or for short bits of dialogue necessary to move on the action. Very often Will deliberately gave prose speeches to his more low-born characters, servants, soldiers and commoners, to differentiate them from nobility and royalty, but this isn't a hard and fast rule.

What is true, however, that Will usually saved his best poetry, for the most dramatic points in the play: speeches of heightened emotion, crises in his characters' lives, watershed moments of sudden insight. Why wouldn't he? He wanted them to stand out in the play. He knew about pulling out all the stops. He also knew about the dramatic effects of contrast, vital in all art forms, be it painting, music, film or literature: light and shade, night and day, happy and sad, funny and serious, fast and slow, whispered or shouted, poetry and prose...

6. Did he mean all the meanings?

The short answer is probably *not all of them!*

If you're studying a section of text, say one of the key speeches, you may find yourself wondering just how consciously Will chose every word, while working at his table, by the light of a flickering taper, over four hundred years ago.

Writers often can't explain how the creative process works for them. There are times when Will's poetry – indeed others' poetry, too – defies total deconstruction or explanation because it's such a concentrated, distilled and subjective form of language, involving different figures of speech and images. We all use imagery, or non-literal language, in speaking and writing at an unconscious level, and it's the most difficult part of language to pin down. Poetry is especially rich in imagery so that multiple meanings fan out; what has one association for someone will take on a whole different significance for someone else. You can be sure that Will was a natural who worked intuitively at times, someone who made it look easy, as only the talented can. This doesn't mean he didn't have to revise or rework at other times... and even Will could have suffered writer's block, when things were going badly.

What *is* certain is that, immersed in the writing of a play, he often used a whole set of images and a whole lexicon of words appropriate for its themes, so that there is a fit between language and content. It's like an artist deciding to paint a picture in a chosen palette of colours. For example, it's not a coincidence that many of the words and images in *Macbeth* are connected with darkness and evil, as in Lady Macbeth's speech:

Come thick night,

And pall thee in the dunnest smoke of Hell,

That my keen knife see not the wound it makes,

Nor Heaven peep through the blanket of the dark,

To cry hold, hold!

There are times when Will Shakespeare's language defies analysis but is resonant on levels way, way deeper than the purely literal. Will was doing things with language that most writers can only dream about.

7. How important was his education?

Very. Put simply, it was crucial to his writing, however much natural talent he had.

Deadly dull, repetitive and harsh, as the learning methods of an Elizabethan grammar school may seem to us today, they gave the pupils a very thorough grounding in the work of the classical writers. It's thought that Will loved some of the poetry he was made to study and probably knew as much about Latin and Greek literature as students today studying for a Master's degree in Classics. This included the chief characteristics of style employed by the Ancients, especially the art of rhetoric, flamboyant, persuasive language, which continued to be highly esteemed in the 16th century. Originally it was developed in the civilizations of Greece and Rome for legal and political purposes, so you could speak eloquently and convince people of your case or cause. Listen to barristers in court or politicians in parliament and you'll find that rhetoric is still alive and well today. Though with the sound-bite mentality of television, it's true to say that the ability to deliver a great speech is valued less today than it was.

Will, of course, was chiefly writing for the stage during his career, but it was still about persuasion and the power to move people, through a drama, which would last on average about two and a half hours in performance. He didn't need a degree in Communication Studies to be aware of the effect of his words on those who flocked to hear them. Gladdened or saddened, depending on the type of play, the spectators would return to their lives, reflecting on the emotional experience. Perhaps they shared it with friends, recalling scenes, and speeches, looking forward to their next visit to *The Curtain, The Rose* or *The Globe*. Some of the more educated might follow up the performance by buying and reading the quarto copies that were being published.

It was always a learning curve for Will Shakespeare, as it is for all creative artists: immersed in the day-to-day life of the theatre, he learnt pretty quickly to adapt his knowledge and reading, and to find a style of his own for plays that would work on the new London stages, including, later on, in the reign of James I, the new indoor theatre at Blackfriars.

8. Do we know how the Elizabethan and Jacobeans spoke?

No. Though researchers have discovered a lot about Elizabethan and Jacobean drama, not to mention all those new theatres breaching the London skyline, we will never hear Shakespeare's language spoken as the Elizabethan audience did. We'll never have that novelty value of watching one of his first performances at the original *Globe,* unless time travel is invented – which it may be, of course. However the first time you see a production of a play by Shakespeare comes the closest to this experience, especially if you haven't read it and don't know the plot.

Those first audiences didn't know, of course, how famous Will was to become, after those epoch-making performances. We, however, are freighted with that knowledge and it can be rather daunting.

But, the upside is that we can now read good editions of all his plays and we can go to the theatre and see productions of most of them. With the help of technology, we can listen to recordings and watch film, TV and DVD versions all in the comfort of our own homes. There is no doubt that watching a play and listening to the words is the best way of understanding Shakespeare's plays.

9. How on earth did he write so much?

I simply don't know.

No-one knows. What keeps going through my brain, as I write, is how, by God's holy trousers, did he produce such poetry when writing against the clock for a performance already in rehearsal or a new play required by the court for the Christmas festivities? Never mind about the need for all the other stuff in his job description and the constant vigilance on the business side. How did he manage to write such soaring verse, such unforgettable lines, such spell-binding poetry to transcend an age of huge inequality and suffering, when life was precarious and short, merely *an hour upon the stage*, to quote Will again?

I simply don't know.

Acknowledgments

I'm extremely grateful to friends and family who've supported me in this venture, listened to me outlining my plans, and tolerated my moaning on about problems. They've said things to help or reassure, and, often, without realising it, triggered ideas or solutions.

A big thank you to my partner, Les, for keeping me positive through many discussions, for being on the same wavelength all the time and for living in the 16/17th centuries with me. Also for vital IT help, and for countless suggestions about content and wording, like the all-important title, *Befriend the Bard!*

Thank-you to my son, Richard, for his dramatic, intuitive drawings and his storyboard take on Will's life.

Thank-you to my friend and fellow English teacher, Isla Matthews, for discussions, insights and shared enthusiasm for the plays of Shakespeare.

And to my friend, Errol Matthews, for the professional help with the psychological profile of Will Shakespeare, the man. (Any misunderstandings about terminology are mine alone.)

And to my friend, Colin Stewart, for his frequent use of mock-Elizabethan expletives, like *God's holy trousers!*

Bibliography

Bate, Jonathan. *The Genius of Shakespeare.* Picador/OUP, 1997

Bate, Jonathan. *Soul of the Age: The Life, Mind and Work of William Shakespeare.* Viking, 2008

Bryson, Bill. *Shakespeare: The World as Stage.* Harper Collins, 2007

Burgess, Anthony. *Shakespeare.* Jonathan Cape, 1970

Burgess, Anthony. *Nothing like the Sun. A Story of Shakespeare's Love Life.* Heinemann 1964

Cook, Judith. *The Roaring Boys.* Sutton Publishing Limited, 2004

Dover Wilson, J. *The Essential Shakespeare.* Cambridge University Press, 1932

Duncan-Jones, Katherine. *Shakespeare: An Ungentle Life.* Bloomsbury, 2010

Edited Paul Edmondson and Stanley Wells. *The Shakespeare Circle.* Cambridge University Press, 2015

Greenblatt, Stephen. *Will in the World: How Shakespeare became Shakespeare.* W.W. Norton & Co.,2004

Holden, Anthony. *William Shakespeare. His Life and Work.* Little, Brown and Company, 1999

Holderness, William. *Nine Lives of William Shakespeare.* Continuum Publishing Group, 2011

Kermode, Frank. *Shakespeare's Language*. Penguin, 2000

Lynch, Jack. *Becoming Shakespeare*. Bloomsbury, 2008

McEvoy, Sean. *Shakespeare: The Basics*. Routledge, 2000

McGregor, Neil. *Shakespeare's Restless World*. Penguin, 2014

Marlowe, Arthur. *Digging for the Truth*. Green & Co., 1978

Mays, Andrea. *The Millionaire and the Bard*. Simon and Schuster, 2015

Muir, Kenneth and Schoenbaum, S. *A New Companion to Shakespeare Studies*. Cambridge University Press, 1971

Nicholl, Charles. *The Lodger: Shakespeare on Silver Street*. Penguin, 2007

Riley, Dick and McAllister, Pam. *The Bedside, Bathtub and Armchair Companion to Shakespeare*. Continuum International Publishing Group, 2001

Sen Gupta, S.C. *A Shakespeare Manual*. OUP, 1977

Shapiro, James. *1599: A Year in the Life of William Shakespeare*. Faber and Faber, 2005

Shapiro, James. *1606: William Shakespeare and the Year of Lear*. Faber and Faber, 2015

Wells, Stanley. *Shakespeare & Co*. Penguin, 2006

Wells, Stanley. *Why Shakespeare WAS Shakespeare*. Kindle Single. 2014

Wells, Stanley. *Shakespeare, Sex and Love*. Oxford University Press. 2010

Wood, Michael. *In Search of Shakespeare*. BBC, 2005

Lightning Source UK Ltd.
Milton Keynes UK
UKOW01f1921041116

286825UK00002B/92/P